ISLAM
A new approach

Jan Thompson

Hodder & Stoughton
A MEMBER OF THE HODDER HEADLINE GROUP

British Library Cataloguing in Publication Data

A catalogue record for this book is
available from the British Library

ISBN 0 340 69778 4

First published 1998
Impression number   10   9   8   7   6
Year   2008, 2007, 2006, 2005, 2004

Typeset by Wearset, Boldon, Tyne and Wear.
Printed in Dubai for Hodder & Stoughton Educational,
a division of Hodder Headline, 338 Euston Road,
London NW1 3BH.

For Nicolas McDowall

Acknowledgements

The publishers would like to thank the following for permission to reproduce copyright material in this volume.

Cheetah Books for the extracts from *Eid Mubarak* by Nadia Bakhsh; The Christian Education Movement for the extract of an interview from *Religious Education Today*, Spring 1988; Alistair Duncan for the extract from his book *Towards Islam*; The Islamic Cultural Centre and London Central Mosque for extracts from a newsletter and a leaflet by Dr Sayyed Darsh; The Islamic Foundation for extracts from *The Muslim Guide* by M. Y. McDermott and M. M. Ahsan; The Muslim Educational Trust for the translations from *Third Primer of Islam* (1973), which has been replaced by *The Children's Book of Salah* by Ghulam Sarwar (1987); Angela Neustatter/Times Newspapers Limited for the extract from her article 'I love Allah. I love Islam', Times Education Supplement, 14 March 1986; The New Internationalist for the extract from *The New Internationalist*, June 1985; Newspaper Publishing Plc for extracts from *The Independent*, 2 May 1988, 16 April 1997 and 17 April 1997; Religious and Moral Education Press for the extract from *Ramadan and Id-Ul-Fitr*, by Janis Hannaford (1982); The Society for Promoting Christian Knowledge for the prayer by Abd al-aziz al-Dirini from 'Purity of Heart' from *Muslim Devotions* translated by Constance E. Padwick; Ta-ha Publishers Limited for the extracts from *The Prophet Muhammad's Last Sermon* translated by Al Bukhari; Times Newspapers Limited for the extracts from 'Early rising on the home front' by William Greaves from *The Times*, 17 August 1987 and 'Mecca: the aftermath' by the Sunday Times Foreign Correspondent from *The Sunday Times*, 9 August 1987.

The publishers would like to thank the following for permission to reproduce copyright photographs in this book:

Circa Photo Library: pp. 5, 33, 37, 54
Circa Photo Library/John Smith: p. 97
Circa Photo Library © William Holtby: pp. 26, 90
Camerapix/COP: pp. 61, 63, 69
Christine Osborne Pictures: pp. 22, 51, 60, 86
Rwar Burton/COP: p. 88
Philip Emmett: p. 102
N. Roberts/COP: p. 78
P. Syder/COP: p. 81
Peter Sanders: pp. 21, 24, 29, 64, 67, 82
Jan Thompson: pp. 2, 52, 89
Mel Thompson: pp. 3, 19, 74

Every effort has been made to acknowledge sources and ownership of copyright. The publishers will be glad to make suitable arrangements with any copyright holders whom it has not been possible to contact.

Cover photograph: Dome of the Rock, Jerusalem. © Christine Osborne Pictures.
Illustrations by Jane Taylor
Maps and diagrams by Tom Cross Illustration

Contents

Author's Notes

Arabic words are spelt in English according to the *Glossary of Terms* published by SCAA in 1994, and recommended to publishers to try to standardise spellings.

English interpretations of the Arabic Qur'an are taken from either *The Koran Interpreted* by A. J. Arberry or *The Meaning of the Glorious Koran* by M. M. Pickthall. These quotations, and also those from the Hadith, appear in special boxes.

CE stands for Common Era and BCE for Before Common Era.

Introduction

Why Study Islam?

Islam is the religion of the Muslims. You have your own reasons, of course, for studying it, but here are some others which you might like to consider if you are looking at the question from a Western point of view.

1   Islam is the fastest-growing religion in the world. After a period of decline over the last three centuries, it is making a come-back and is now second only to Christianity in size. At least a sixth of the people of the world are Muslims. Some would claim that the figure is much higher: one in five, or even a quarter of the world's population. It is not easy to know exactly, but 800 million is a conservative estimate.

    It is surely worth discovering why this religion is so popular.

2   In Britain too, Islam is a religion which cannot be ignored. The first British mosque was built in Woking in Surrey, in 1889. In 1965 there were only 13 mosques in Britain. But in the following 20 years, with the number of Muslims in this country steadily growing, over 300 mosques were opened. A century after the first mosque was built in Britain, the Islamic Cultural Centre reported an estimated figure of over 400 mosques (many of which are not purpose-built).

    With up to two million Muslims in Britain, Islam is now its second-largest religion. (Statistics vary because census data do not include religious affiliation.) These Muslims include those who have come to Britain as students and on business, as well as the families which have settled here – at least a third of whom were born here and know no other home.

    The study of Islam is therefore important, if we are to understand and show respect for our Muslim neighbours.

3   Business people must learn to deal with Muslims internationally. The oil wealth of many Muslim countries has given them power to affect the Western economy.

4   It is necessary to know about Islam in order to understand world affairs. A headline in a daily newspaper (July 1988) read: 'Ceasefire is God's will, says Khomeini'. It is a reminder that Iran is an Islamic country, ruled by religious leaders.

What world affairs are in the news at the moment, involving Muslims?

5   If you already have a grounding in Christianity and Judaism, then you will find Islam quite easy to understand. All three religions worship one God; Muslims use the name **Allah** which is Arabic for 'the God'. All claim to go back to Abraham. When you read the **Qur'an**, the holy book of Islam, you will recognise characters mentioned in both the Old and New Testaments of the Bible.

6   If you are not a Muslim, the study of Islam is bound to challenge some of your own beliefs and values. In looking at those which are different from your own, you will see things in a new light. You will be encouraged both to evaluate the importance of Islamic beliefs for Muslims, and also to state your own opinions. Are you ready for that challenge?

1

The Mosque

A mosque is a Muslim place of worship. It is called a **masjid** in Arabic, the language of Islam. This word literally means 'place of prostration' because, strictly speaking, a mosque is anywhere a Muslim kneels down to prostrate him or herself in prayer. A prayer-mat laid down at home, or even at the side of the road, becomes a mosque – a place of prostration.

We can learn a lot about Islam by studying mosques, starting with this name masjid, describing the Muslim practice of prostrating themselves when they pray. It is an act of complete surrender to **Allah** (the Muslim name for God). A **Muslim** is, literally, 'one who surrenders' to Allah, and the word **islam** means 'surrender'. Islam also means 'peace' because it comes from the Arabic 'to make peace' (which is done by making an act of surrender). Muslims believe that true peace of mind can only come from submission to Allah's will, since they believe he is the Creator and knows what is best for all of his creation.

Once a place is set aside for use as a mosque, then it is subject to a number of rules. Congregational prayers must be held there five times a day, and Muslims must be clean when they enter the mosque. This is because the building is regarded as belonging to Allah.

External Features

It may be difficult to recognise mosques in non-Muslim countries because, for example, they may be converted houses, redundant church buildings or even fire stations. The only distinguishing feature on the outside may be the notice-board. Those which are purpose-built, however, will probably have the traditional external features of a domed roof and minaret. Some elaborate mosques have many domes and minarets. What are they for, and what do they tell us about Islam?

The Dome

This is an important feature of buildings in hot countries because it allows the air to circulate. Islam comes from the Middle East, where the climate is very hot. The dome is built over the prayer hall as it also helps to amplify the human voice.

The Minaret

This is a tall tower. In Muslim countries the call to prayer five times a day comes from the top of the minaret. This call rings out over the roofs of other buildings. It is like an alarm clock, reminding people when it is time to pray. Regular daily prayer is obviously very important in Islam. Originally, a man called a **muezzin** would climb the tower each time, to give the prayer call. Now recordings and loudspeakers tend to be used.

Internal Features

A mosque has three uses: it is a place of worship, an Islamic school or college, and a

Mosques can be recognised by their domes and minarets.

community centre. Its rooms and facilities must meet all these needs.

The Prayer Hall

The most important part of a mosque, the prayer hall, is often something of a disappointment to visitors as there is not much to see. **Masjid** literally means 'place of prostration', and the prayer hall is simply a large space for the men to gather for prayer. In hot countries this might just be an open courtyard. There are no seats because room is needed to go through the prayer movements.

The Women's Worship Area

Women do not have to attend mosques, and often their family responsibilities will prevent them from doing so. If they do attend, they will worship and prepare for worship separately from the men, so that the two sexes do not distract each other. Often there is a balcony at the back of the prayer hall for the women. Their worship area will be smaller than the men's, since fewer women attend mosques.

Washing Facilities

People do not want to prostrate themselves on a dirty floor, so it is important to keep the prayer hall clean. This is also done out of respect for Allah. Outdoor shoes are removed before entering and left in the shoe-racks provided. Visitors do not have to wash before going into a mosque, but Muslims going there to pray have to wash thoroughly beforehand. Facilities must be provided for this. If there are washrooms there will be separate ones for men and women or, in hot countries, there may be two separate fountains or taps in the courtyard.

Carpeting

Some Muslims will use individual prayer mats, but the prayer hall will be carpeted anyway, so that it is comfortable to walk on in bare feet, and to sit and kneel on.

The prayer mat usually has an arch design on it, so that the mat can be laid down in the correct direction for prayer, pointing towards the Ka'bah in Makkah, the holy city of Islam. The one shown has a picture of the Ka'bah placed centrally in the top half. This large, cube-shaped building stands in the centre of the Sacred Mosque in Makkah. The Qur'an states that Muhammad, the supreme prophet of Islam, worshipped here.

Sometimes mosques have special carpeting that has been designed to look like lots of individual prayer mats; and the carpet is laid so that the arches point towards the Ka'bah. This direction is called the **qiblah**.

The Mihrab

Muslims will know the qiblah as all mosques have a **mihrab**, which is an alcove in the wall. If Muslims face it when they pray, they will be facing in the direction of the Ka'bah. It also serves the useful purpose of amplifying the voice of the **imam** who leads the prayers, facing in the correct direction, with his back to the rest of the worshippers.

The Minbar

The only piece of furniture required in a mosque is the **minbar**. This is a set of at least three steps to raise the person (usually the imam) who preaches the Friday midday sermon, so that he can be seen and heard. In large mosques the minbar may be very high, with a small platform on the top.

Decoration

Some mosques are beautifully decorated with intricate patterns; others are plain. In either case, there will be no pictures or statues, because of the risk of idolatry. Islam teaches that Allah is too great to be portrayed by human hands, and therefore forbids any images of him. Decoration on the walls of the mosques often takes the form of beautiful writing (calligraphy) of passages from the Islamic holy book, the Qur'an, which Muslims believe to be Allah's words.

Activities

Key Elements

1. What is a mosque?
2. What is the literal meaning of the word **masjid**?
3. Why do Muslims prostrate themselves when they pray?
4. What two special features are often seen on the outside of a mosque?
5. What is the only piece of furniture to be found in the prayer-hall?
6. Explain the purpose of the alcove in one of the walls.
7. Why do people remove their shoes before entering a mosque?
8. Why are there separate areas in mosques for men and women?
9. What is calligraphy?
10. Why are there no statues or pictures of people or animals in mosques?

Think About It

11 Do you think it is necessary to have somewhere special in order to worship God?

12 Do you think Muslims in non-Muslim countries should feel free to pray in the street and to give the call to prayer from their minarets, as they do in Muslim countries?

13 Do you think Muslims are right to separate men and women in the mosques?

Regular Activities at a Mosque

We have said that a mosque has three basic purposes: a place of worship; an Islamic education centre; and a centre for the Muslim community. Below are some of the 'Regular Activities' advertised for the Islamic Cultural Centre at the London Central Mosque, some of which require special rooms and offices (such as a mortuary, where the dead are brought and prepared for burial).

Regular Activities Held at the Islamic Cultural Centre, London Central Mosque

Educational

Weekend School

Islamic and Arabic classes for children between the ages of 5 and 15 are held on weekends. Children can either attend on Saturdays or Sundays from 10 a.m. to 3 p.m. For further information contact Shaikh Gamal Manna or Mr Aman. There is a Parent/Teacher Association which is actively involved in assisting the school.

Arabic Classes for Adults

These are held every Sunday from 3 to 5 p.m. The classes are taught by Mr Tijani who may be contacted for information on enrolment.

Social and Welfare

Counselling

The Imams of the Centre are Shaikh Gamal Manna, Shaikh Muhammad Zahran and Shaikh Hamid Halifa. They are available at the Centre to discuss any personal problems and difficulties which individual Muslims may have. The Imams are normally available from 10 a.m. to 3 p.m. every weekday except Tuesdays and Fridays.

Marriages

During the month the number of marriages solemnised was twenty.

Visits to Prisons

Delegated imams and persons from the Jamaat (the congregation) visit prison inmates to provide instruction in Islam and perform rehabilitation work. The Centre provides free Islamic literature to them.

Hospital Visits

The Centre would welcome volunteers to visit patients in hospital. Interested persons are asked to contact the Director.

Other Facilities

The Library

The library of the Centre on the upper floor has a wide selection of books and magazines in English, Arabic and other languages. It is only used as a reference library. It is open during normal office hours excepting Saturdays.

Bookshop

The Bookshop has a wide selection of books in Arabic and English on Islam. Audio cassette recordings of the Qur'an are also available.

Funeral Services

The Centre now runs its own funeral service … Expenses are kept to a minimum and must be borne by the estate or relatives of the deceased.

Orientation for Police

Every fortnight new recruits from the Paddington Green Police Station come to listen to a talk from one of the Centre's staff members on Islam.

The British Muslim Association

Meets regularly every Sunday at 3 p.m.

(ICC Newsletter, No. 36)

Rules for Visiting a Mosque

The best way to study mosques is to visit them and talk to the people there. Big centres, like the London Central Mosque, are accustomed to schools visiting them, and issue the following guidelines. You will learn a lot from local mosques, too.

VISITS TO THE MOSQUE AND ISLAMIC CULTURAL CENTRE

1 All visits are accompanied by a guide.

2 Visitors are reminded that the Mosque is a place of worship and they are asked to behave accordingly.

3 As you may be aware it is customary for Muslim women and girls to wear a head cover in the Mosque. It would be appreciated if the appropriate members of your group could wear a scarf or similar head-covering during the visit.

4 We would appreciate it if ladies would wear long sleeved garments of a suitable length (or loose fitting trousers).

5 Before entering the Prayer Hall you will be asked to remove your shoes.

6 Smoking is prohibited in the Mosque and surrounding areas.

7 No alcoholic drinks are allowed on the premises.

8 A complete tour of the Mosque usually takes about 20 minutes and a further 20 or 30 minutes may be devoted to a talk about Islam followed by discussion. The question-time may be prolonged occasionally depending upon the number of questions from the visitors.

9 There is no fee attached to the visits.

10 We are not able to provide resource packs or worksheets. Some schools prepare their own questionnaires prior to their visits. This proves to be very useful during the discussion that follows the tour of the Mosque. Some free leaflets and booklets on Islam are available on request.

11 We find it most convenient to accommodate visits between 10 a.m.–4 p.m., Monday–Thursday.

London Central Mosque.

The Imam

The Arabic word **imam** means 'in the front'. This describes the main purpose of the imam, who is the man who stands in front of the lines of worshippers, leading them in recital of the set prayers.

An imam has no special training, and he is not ordained as a holy man. There are no priests or monks in Islam, all Muslims being regarded as equal in the sight of Allah. Basically, an imam is an educated person who is chosen by the congregation because he is regarded as a good Muslim and because of his knowledge of Islam and ability to recite the Qur'an properly. Some imams are specially trained at Islamic colleges called Dar al-Ulooms, where students follow a seven year course in Arabic and Islamic studies.

Apart from leading the prayers, imams often take on other tasks, as the religious leaders of the local Muslim communities. They often act as the **khatib**, the person who preaches the Friday sermon (the **khutbah**). They will teach about Islam to people of all ages, but particularly to the children who need to learn to read the Qur'an in Arabic. They sometimes perform religious ceremonies, and they will give people religious advice. You will see from the 'Regular Activities at a Mosque' (p. 4) that they are also involved in prison visits. In small mosques the imam may well take on these religious responsibilities as well as another job; in big mosques imams are usually employed full time.

The following interview with Imam Abdul Jalid Sajid, the Imam and Director of the Brighton Islamic Centre and Mosque, gives an insight into his work.

Imam, could you tell us about your upbringing?

I was born and grew up in rural Pakistan. . . . My family wanted me to enter government administration so I went to a school where both the religious and secular traditions were taught. I then studied Arabic, including Islam studies, at Punjab University. From there I went to Dacca University to study both Journalism and Political Science. I became a journalist and also taught

Political Studies at a Christian College. In 1974 I was appointed as a full-time lecturer in Political Studies at Punjab University. It was from there that I came to Britain to do a doctorate.

From this background how did you become an imam?

I had no intention of becoming an imam. Having the qualifications, I was often asked to give sermons at the Friday prayers wherever I happened to be. When I came to Britain in 1976 to the LSE, I joined the Islamic Society and discovered that there was no one qualified to give the khutbah (the formal Arabic sermon). So I gave it every Friday. While doing my studies I also edited a Muslim newsletter and taught children, again because there was no one else. In 1977, at the request of the Brighton Student Group, I started travelling to Brighton every Friday to lead the prayer and give the sermon. All of this was on a voluntary basis. Then, in 1980, two years after my wife had joined me, I was appointed as the full-time Imam and Director here and gave up the idea of a lectureship. There was a great need in Brighton and I felt that God was calling me to do this work.

Apart from leading the Friday prayers, what do you do as an imam?

A tremendous amount! Amongst other things, I organise many activities: educational and religious programmes at the mosque, financial and building projects, an Islamic school for children each evening and midweek classes for other groups. I visit many schools in the area, and speak to many non-Muslim groups. I am also the authorised Muslim prison and hospital chaplain for Sussex.

What is your aim as an imam in a non-Muslim society?

Muslims are a part of British society, which has to realise that it is a multi-faith and multi-cultural society. We must play a full part in this society, always displaying sensitivity, mutual respect and tolerance. Therefore, apart from helping my own community become better Muslims, I see my role as making Islam understood better among non-Muslims, and helping Muslims understand better other religions and ideas. I have spoken in churches and synagogues in the area and this has been reciprocated.

(RE Today)

Activities

Key Elements

1 What are the three main purposes of a mosque?
2 What do Muslim children learn at a mosque school?
3 Which of the 'Regular activities' listed would require an extra room at the mosque, in addition to the prayer-hall?
4 What community services are run by the mosque?
5 Why is it best for non-Muslims *not* to visit a mosque on a Friday?
6 Describe the position of the **imam** when he leads the prayers.
7 Why does the imam need to be an educated man?
8 Why is it wrong to speak of an imam as a priest?

Think About It

9 How do you think non-Muslims can show respect when visiting a mosque?
10 Do you think it is important for religious leaders to be set apart from ordinary people in some way, or is it better if they are just like one of us?

Further Information

The Star and Crescent

Sometimes the dome and minaret of the mosque have a moon-shaped crescent on top of them, or a star and crescent. This five-pointed star and crescent is a symbol of Islam, depicted on the flags and stamps of many Muslim countries.

- The five-pointed star symbolises the Five Pillars of Islam, i.e. the five basic duties of Muslims.
- The moon and stars are signs to Muslims of the greatness of the Creator.

You will learn that Muhammad (the greatest prophet of Islam) and his early followers were desert people. For them the new moon marked the beginning of each new month, and the waxing and waning moon told them what time of the month it was. A new day started, not at midnight but in the evening, with the appearance of the moon. Islam still uses this lunar calendar.

The positions of the stars were used for guidance by desert people who travelled when it was cool at night and rested in the heat of the day. Stars were also used for finding the direction of **Makkah**, the holy city of Islam. Astronomy became an important Islamic science; with the minaret as an ideal astronomical observatory. By the tenth century Muslims had invented the astrolabe, an instrument with which they calculated the movements of stars and planets. They were able to tell the time of night from this – the forerunner of our clock.

Questions

- How does the Islamic year differ from the Western year?
- Find out how an astrolabe works.
- Discover which countries have the star and crescent on their flags, then draw them.

Further Information

Islamic Art

The first and highest art form in Islam is calligraphy because it is used to write out passages from the Qur'an and decorate the mosques. This beautiful writing is done in different styles, but even in its most elaborate forms, where the Arabic is very difficult to read, it is a reminder to the faithful of the importance of Allah's words.

The second most important art form is architecture, because this is used to design mosques, as well as other buildings.

Third and finally are either the geometric designs, or the fascinating interweaving of leaves in a floral pattern, known as arabesque. These too are used to decorate mosques, among other things. The harmony of these intricate designs speaks to believers of the order and balance in Allah's universe and of the unity intended for humanity.

Of least importance in Islam is figurative art. There are a number of reasons for this:

- Muhammad denounced the makers of images and pictures, although they are not forbidden in the Qur'an.
- Idolatry is considered the worst sin in Islam, so anything which could lead to it is avoided. There is a strict prohibition against any representation of the human form in mosques and many Muslims have taken this more generally.
- Muslims are taught that they should not usurp Allah's creative role. Therefore, if they depict any parts of nature, such as a plant, they must make it two-dimensional and highly stylised, rather than trying to make it look like the real thing which Allah created.

However, these rules about figurative art are taken more strictly by some Muslims than others. For example, the Persians continued to paint miniatures, even after their conversion to Islam. So it is possible to find some pictures of Muslim figures, even of Muhammad.

Draw a 5 cm square.
Divide it into a grid of 1 cm squares.
Add lines.

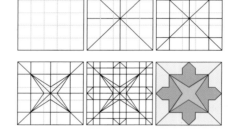

Take away lines

This leaves the final design

Make a larger pattern using the final design as a repeating unit.

Patterns from *The Eid-ul-Fitr Book*, p. 85.

Islamic decorative pattern, with Arabic writing in the centre.

Activities

- Find books of geometric patterns in Islamic book shops, or elsewhere. Colouring these patterns will help you appreciate the way they flow. Choose popular Muslim colours, e.g. greens, blues and golds.

- Study some examples of Islamic patterns, then try to design a simple narrow border.

- The diagrams show how Muslim patterns can be designed within a square. You could also draw a circle inside a square, dividing it into equal segments. Try to design a pattern of your own.

Vocabulary

Give the Arabic words for the following:

1 mosque
2 one who surrenders (to Allah) — a follower of Islam
3 the tower attached to a mosque
4 the person who gives the prayer call
5 the preaching platform
6 the direction for Islamic prayer
7 the alcove in the wall, showing the direction for prayer
8 the prayer leader
9 the preacher of the Friday sermon
10 the Friday sermon

Assignments

1 A Mosque

Either:

a) Convert your classroom into a room suitable as a simple mosque.

b) Make a note of all the alterations necessary and the reasons for these.

c) If it were to become a permanent mosque, which other parts of your school might be useful to have as part of the mosque, and why?

Or:

a) Make a model, or draw a plan, of a mosque (remembering that it must serve a variety of uses). Write a key to it, naming all the rooms and features.

b) Explain the religious purposes of all the parts of your mosque.

c) How important do you think it is, for Muslims living in non-Muslim countries, to have a mosque within easy reach?

2   Visiting a mosque

Using the 'Rules for Visiting a Mosque' (p. 5):

a) Write a notice, suitable for display at the entrance to a mosque, telling people what they must do before entering and what rules they should observe there.

b) Explain the Islamic reasons for Rules 3–7. You will have to find out the Islamic attitude to women's dress and drugs (smoking and alcohol) from Chapter 8.

c) Read Rule 2. What do you consider to be appropriate behaviour for a visitor to a place of worship?

3   The Imam

a) Write an advertisement for a full-time imam at a local mosque, describing what he will be expected to do.

b) Imagine you know someone who has applied for this job, whom you con-sider to be an ideal person for it. Write a reference for him, explaining in what ways he is suitable.

c) Assuming your friend is appointed, how important do you think his work will be in the community?

2

Prayer

Prayer Timetable

The alarm clock rang at 4.30 a.m. and, as usual, it was Purveen who answered its summons. In the bathroom of the family's three-bedroom, terraced house in Southall, Middlesex, she embarked on the ritual of wudu, *cleaning teeth, nose, mouth, ears, hands and forearms and, lastly her feet. Ready now to perform the* Fajr *prayer, she returned to the bedroom, faced towards the shrine of Kaaba in Mecca, made her* Niyyah *– the announcement of her intention to pray – read a paragraph from the Qur'an and prostrated herself to Allah.*

With a great deal of door banging, shouting and cajoling, Purveen succeeded in raising daughters, Amberin and Zarrin, sons Saad and Yousef and, last of all, her husband from the depths of their slumbers. As an architect with Ealing Borough Council, Ghayas Syed was not due at work until after nine o'clock and, left to themselves, his family would not be disposed to such spectacular early rising. Indeed, within an hour of the alarm ringing, all of them were back in bed and sound asleep.

Like all devout Muslims, however, the Syeds adhere rigidly to the timetable of prayers which is the centrepiece of their faith. There would be four more prayer sessions to be slotted into the Syed family schedule during the day.

(William Greaves in The Times)

Perhaps this makes prayer sound like a terrible burden; but I have also heard a Muslim liken the prayer times to tea-breaks. We look forward to the breaks in our daily routine and the chance for refreshment and relaxation. In the same way, prayer times clear the mind of immediate concerns like a Maths problem, an English assessment or the demands of a job. By washing for prayer, Muslims are refreshed; through the physical actions of prayer, they are relaxed. Most important of all, they can bring their minds back to focus on Allah who is, for them, the reason and purpose of their existence.

Notice that the newspaper article says 'the timetable of prayers . . . is the centrepiece of their faith'. There are five things which are obligatory (**fard**) for a Muslim, known as the Five Pillars of Islam. The first of these is to declare their belief in Allah and in Muhammad his Prophet. Next is **salah**, ritual prayer, to be performed five times a day. In this way, Muslims regularly declare their faith in Allah and offer him praise.

Times of Salah

*So glory be to God
  both in your evening hour
  and in your morning hour.
His is the praise
  in the heavens and earth,
  alike at the setting sun
  and in your noontide hour.*

(Arberry)   *(Qur'an 30:17–18)*

*Proclaim thy Lord's praise
  before the rising of the sun, and before its
  setting, and
  proclaim thy Lord's praise
  in the watches of the night, and at the ends
  of the day.*

(Arberry)   *(Qur'an 20:130)*

The five daily prayers are not laid down in any one passage of the Qur'an, although they can be reached by putting these two passages together. It was left to Muhammad to give more precise details as to their times, and these are found in the *Hadith*, which record what Muhammad said and did.

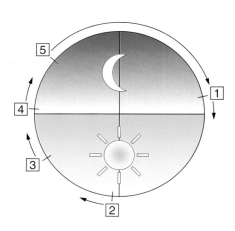

1 **Fajr** – the morning prayer, between dawn and sunrise.

2 **Zuhr** – after midday, during the early afternoon.

3 **Asr** – the late afternoon prayer.

4 **Maghrib** – just after sunset.

5 **Isha** – the night prayer.

Notice that the times are not set *exactly* at sunrise, noon or sunset, to avoid any suggestion of sun worship. However they are still *related* to the sun, which changes with the seasons, so they are not always at the same time each day throughout the year. It is important, therefore, for Muslims to know the times of sunrise and sunset each day.

The prayer sessions are quite short, and can take place at any time during the correct periods. If, for any good reason, Muslims are unable to say the prayers at their correct times, then they may say a number of prayers together at the next correct time; however, prayers are not allowed to be said in advance.

Ibn Mas'ud reported: I asked the Messenger of Allah (peace and blessings of Allah be upon him), 'Which deed is the most desirable to Allah?' He replied: 'To offer the obligatory prayer in time.'

(Selection from Hadith, No. 27, p. 17)

Friday Prayer

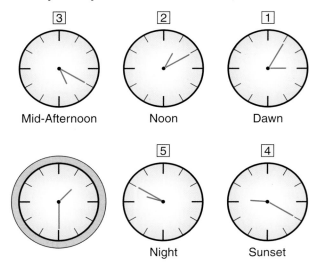

Mosques have to decide on the times when they will hold the prayers, for people who are able to come and say them there rather than at home or at work. You might be surprised to see *six* clock faces, showing the times of prayer at a mosque. The sixth one shows the time of the special Friday service, when the

Jumu'ah prayer takes the place of the **Zuhr** prayer. *Jumu'ah* is Arabic for 'assembly' or 'congregation'; and Friday, the holy day for Muslims, is called *Yaum ul-Jumu'ah*, the Day of Assembly. All Muslim men should attend mosque on that day, around noon, to join in the congregational prayer and listen to the sermon (the **khutbah**). Women are not obliged to attend because of their domestic duties.

> *O ye who believe! When the call is heard for the prayer of the day of congregation, haste unto remembrance of Allah and leave your trading. That is better for you if ye did but know.*
>
> *(Pickthall)*   *(Qur'an 62:9)*

Call to Prayer

Muslims are called to prayer five times a day by the **muezzin**, who stands facing the Ka'bah. In Muslim countries this call goes out from the top of the minarets, and is broadcast on radio and television. In non-Muslim countries it is usual for the call only to be given *inside* the mosque, warning those who have gathered there that prayer is about to begin.

This picture shows a muezzin calling from the top of a minaret. More often these days, his voice is on a recording and it is amplified through loud-speakers.

The **adhan** is the first call to prayer. It is in Arabic; but here is an English translation:

> *'Allah is the Greatest.'* (called four times)
> *'I bear witness that there is no god but Allah.'* (twice)
> *'I bear witness that Muhammad is the Messenger of Allah.'* (twice)
> *'Come to prayer.'* (twice)
> *'Come to what is good for you.'* (twice)
> *'Prayer is better than sleep.'* (twice, but only for morning prayer)
> *'Allah is the Greatest.'* (twice)
> *'There is no god but Allah.'*

The adhan is announced in plenty of time for people to prepare themselves for prayer at the mosque, if they are going to attend. Then a second call is given by the muezzin as he stands in the front row of worshippers inside the prayer hall. This is called the **'iqamah** and it warns people that prayer is about to start. It has the same words as the adhan, with the addition of 'Prayer is about to begin'. This is said twice after 'Come to what is good for you'. All other lines are said only once this time, apart from 'Allah is the Greatest', which is repeated.

Preparations for Prayer

Muslims must be properly dressed for prayer. This means removing their shoes, and being cleanly and decently dressed. Women will therefore cover their bodies and wear a scarf over their heads, leaving only their faces and hands uncovered. Men must be covered from at least the waist to the knees. They do not have to wear anything on their heads, but it is customary to wear a prayer-cap, which holds the hair in place during prostrations.

Activities

Key Elements

1 When are the five prayer times?
2 Why are Islamic prayers *not* at sunrise, noon and sunset?
3 On which day of the week is the Muslim Day of Assembly?
4 What does the sixth clock-face show, at a mosque?
5 Can you think of any reasons, particularly for Muslims living in non-Muslim countries, why they might not be able to perform the prayers at the correct times?
6 Using the following Hadith, explain why it is particularly important for Muslims to pray at the beginning and the end of each day.

Ibn 'Umar reported that the Messenger of Allah (peace and blessings of Allah be upon him) said: 'To offer the prayer in the first hour is to please God and to offer the prayer in late hours is to ask for Allah's pardon.'

(Jami' Al-Tirmizi; Selection from Hadith, No. 28, p. 17)

7 The Qur'an says 'Prayer restrains from shameful and unjust deeds' (29:45). (*The Essential Teachings of Islam p90*). Explain why it should have this effect.
8 Who gives the call to prayer from the minaret?
9 What are the differences between the **adhan** and the **'iqamah**?

Think About It

10 If someone believes in prayer, do you think they should do it on a regular basis or just when they feel the need? Answer as fully as possible.

Ritual Washing Before Prayer

Muslims must wash in a particular way before prayer to make themselves ritually clean. This washing is called **wudu** and the procedure is shown in the diagrams that follow.

1 First the hands are washed thoroughly.

2 The mouth is rinsed out three times.

3 Water is snuffed into the nose and blown out, three times.

6 Wet hands are run backwards over the head, turned over to wipe the neck, and brought round to wipe the ears, inside and out.

4 All parts of the face are then washed three times, using both hands.

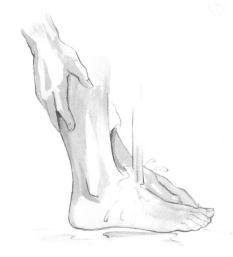

7 The right foot, then the left, are washed thoroughly up to the ankle.

5 The right arm, then the left, are washed from wrist to elbow, three times.

Before performing wudu a Muslim will say 'In the name of Allah, the Compassionate, the Merciful'. When he has finished he will make the declaration of faith, 'I bear witness that there is no god but Allah, and Muhammad is the Messenger of Allah'.

Prayer Positions

Salah consists of set words which are recited from memory, led by the imam. These are mostly expressions of praise for Allah and quotations from the Qur'an. These words are accompanied by set actions; this cycle of ritual prayers and postures is called a **rak'ah**. Each of the five salah requires a particular number of these units, as follows:

- **Fajr** – 2
- **Zuhr** – 4
- **Asr** – 4
- **Maghrib** – 3
- **Isha** – 4

It is best to see salah for yourself (perhaps on video), for the full impact of the flow of the Arabic words and movements. But the diagrams that follow will help you to think about the significance of each position.

Muslims face in the direction of the Ka'bah when they pray. If they are in a strange place, this direction, the **qiblah**, can be found by using a special Islamic compass. If they are at a mosque, they will line up, shoulder to shoulder (men with men and women with women), facing the mihrab, and behind the imam.

> *We have seen the turning of thy face to heaven (for guidance, O Muhammad). And now verily we shall make thee turn (in prayer) toward a qiblah which is dear to thee. So turn thy face toward the Inviolable Place of Worship, and ye (O Muslims), wheresoever ye may be, turn your faces (when ye pray) toward it.*
>
> *(Pickthall)*   *(Qur'an 2:144)*

The Muslim begins prayer by saying to him- or herself that he or she intends to offer this salah. This intention, called **niyyah**, is a conscious effort to focus the mind on Allah and to do the prayer for him. Everything is said in Arabic, but English translations (from *Third Primer of Islam*, pp. 14–22) are given below.

1   She raises her hands briefly to her ears, with the words 'Allahu Akbar' ('Allah is the Greatest'). There is the idea in this gesture of putting behind her all other concerns – only Allah remains before her.

2   In this next position, she says:
    'O Allah, Glorified, praiseworthy and blessed is Thy name and exalted Thy Majesty and there is no deity worthy of worship except Thee. I seek refuge in Allah from the rejected Satan.'
The opening chapter of the Qur'an is then recited (sometimes silently), followed by another passage from the Qur'an during the first two rak'ahs.

3 Bowing, as a sign of respect, she says 'Allahu Akbar' and then, three times, 'Glory to my Lord the great'.

4 While standing upright, which is also a sign of respect, she says: 'Allah has heard all who praise him. Our Lord: Praise be to Thee.'

5 With the words 'Allahu Akbar', she prostrates herself on the ground and says three times 'Glory to my Lord, the most high.' After sitting back on her heels for a moment, she repeats this. This position is called **sajdah**, and shows the Muslim's complete submission before Allah. This is very significant because the word 'Islam' means both 'submission' and 'peace'. This shows the Muslim belief that inner peace and outward harmony can only

come from all God's creatures submitting to his laws.

The first rak'ah is now complete. It takes only about a minute to do.

Note the three basic positions: standing (**qiyam**), bowing (**ruku**), and prostrating (**sajdah**). Each of these goes further than the one before it in showing submission to Allah.

6 After the second rak'ah, she sits back with the left foot bent towards the right one, as shown, and her hands on her knees. In this position, she silently recites further prayers, particularly asking Allah's blessing on Muhammad and Ibrahim.

7 When the correct number of rak'ahs are completed, she turns her head to the right and then to the left, blessing her fellow Muslims each time with the words, 'Peace be on you and Allah's blessings.' This is called **salam**, which means 'peace'.

Personal Prayer

This chapter has concentrated on **salah**, the obligatory prayers, with set words and set forms, which are recited five times a day. There is also **du'a**, personal prayer. This Arabic word literally means 'asking' and, like any believer, Muslims will have special concerns to bring to Allah in prayer, over and above the prayers laid down for them.

Du'a can take various forms. The worshipper can stay seated after salah and say his own prayers in his own language, or recite some Arabic prayers. Or he can do additional rak'ahs. Du'a can be the prayers said by individual Muslims, in their own words, at any time of day. It can be the recitation of the Qur'an while going about one's work. It can be the repetition of prayers on prayer-beads.

> *O ye who believe! Seek help in steadfastness and prayer.*
>
> *(Pickthall)*   *(Qur'an 2:153)*

Activities

Key Elements

1   The exposed parts of the body are washed in wudu. What are they?
2   Why is niyyah (intention) important before prayer?
3   What do Muslims wear for prayer?
4   Find out how an Islamic compass works. (They can be bought separately or are sometimes attached to a prayer-mat.) Which direction is Makkah from your home-town?
5   Explain the significance of all Muslims in the world turning to face the Ka'bah when they pray.
6   What are the three main prayer positions, in the order in which they are done?
7   What does the position called sajdah signify, and why do Muslims say 'Allahu Akbar' as they prostrate themselves?
8   Muslims pray with their bodies as well as with words and thoughts. What does this tell us about the Muslim attitude to prayer?
9   When Muslims pray together, they fill up each line from the front of the mosque, standing shoulder to shoulder. What does this show about their attitude to each other?

Think About It

10   What difference do you think it makes to the quality of prayer if a person has taken the trouble to prepare for it properly?
11   What value can you see in repeating an important phrase over and over?
12   What are the advantages and disadvantages for a Muslim in attending congregational prayer, rather than praying on his or her own?

Further Information

Ritual Washing

- It is not necessary for Muslims to repeat wudu between prayers if they remain in a state of ritual cleanliness. However, they are no longer clean if they go to the toilet or fall asleep.
- If, after performing wudu, the person does anything to make them impure, such as passing wind or going to the toilet, then the wudu must be repeated.
- A full bath is sometimes necessary before prayer, such as after a wet dream or sexual intercourse.
- If there is no water available for wudu, dry cleaning of the hands, face and arms is an alternative. This is done by touching dust or sand with both hands and then wiping the face and the arms up to the elbows (once).

Further Information

Prayer-beads

Muslim prayer-beads are called **subhah**, but are also known by the rarer term, **misbahah**. Some Muslims refer to the beads as **tasbih**

but, strictly speaking, this describes the action of using beads rather than the beads themselves.

The beads are threaded quite loosely on the string, and the ends are knotted together, often finishing in a tassle. The telling of prayer-beads is done by passing each bead through the thumb and forefinger, to keep count of the prayers.

Each string has 33 or 99 beads (the latter is divided into sets of 33 by three 'rogue' beads). These are used to recite the Ninety Nine Beautiful Names. These are 99 different attributes of Allah which occur in the Qur'an, such as 'the Compassionate', and 'the Merciful'.

Not all Muslims use prayer-beads, but they are particularly important in **Sufism**, which is the mystical movement in Islam. Sufis use the beads to repeat a sacred formula hundreds or thousands of times. Sufism has had a strong influence on Islam generally, and many Muslims use strings of beads to repeat phrases about Allah. On the first 33 beads they repeat 'Subhan Allah', the Arabic for 'Glory be to Allah'; on the next 33 they say 'al-hamdu-li-Llah', which means 'All praise be to Allah'; and lastly, they say 'Allahu Akbar', 'Allah is the Greatest', 33 times, and once more on the end piece.

Muslims who go on pilgrimage to Makkah can buy special black and white prayer-beads there.

Questions
- Make a set of prayer-beads for a display on Islam.
- What value can you see in repeating an important phrase over and over?
- Explain how the use of prayer-beads can encourage discipline and concentration in prayer.

Vocabulary

Give the Arabic words for the following:

1 ritual prayer
2 'assembly'; name for the Friday prayer
3 name of the first call to prayer
4 name of the second call to prayer
5 ritual washing before prayer
6 a cycle of prayers and movements; one unit of salah
7 the building towards which Muslims face when they pray
8 intention (to pray)
9 'Allah is the Greatest'
10 personal prayer

Assignment

1 Salah

a) Find out the times of sunrise and sunset from a daily newspaper. Then draw five clock-faces and mark on them possible times for today's five daily prayers. (For the night-prayer, put your usual bed-time.) Under each clock, put the Arabic name for the prayer.

b) Think of all the benefits derived from wudu and explain them. Include those benefits which you may not regard as particularly 'religious', since Islam makes no distinction between 'religious' and 'non-religious' – it teaches people to live their whole lives for Allah.

c) The adhan states that 'prayer is better than sleep'. Is this true? Try to find some people, of any religion, who get up early to pray. Work out a few questions to ask them, and record your questions and their answers. (A local church may be able to help, if you have no Muslim neighbours.)

3

Muhammad

Introduction

By now you will have realised that Muhammad is a key figure in Islam. The first Pillar of Islam is the declaration of faith:

> *There is no god but Allah,*
> *and Muhammad is the Messenger of Allah.*

Islam teaches that there were other prophets before him, but that Muhammad had the last word: that he brought the final, perfect revelation from God to humankind.

When Muslims utter his name, they usually bless him with the words, 'Peace be upon him'. So he was aptly named 'Muhammad', since it means 'the Blessed One' or 'the Praised One'. Muslims look back on Muhammad as the ideal man, and they try to live up to his example of faith and goodness. Most Muslims, out of respect, will not represent Muhammad in any way. Pictures which do exist of Muhammad usually show his face veiled and a large flame-shaped light behind his head. This is similar to the idea of the halo of light, in Christian tradition, to denote a particularly holy person.

For all his importance, Muhammad is not seen as the founder of Islam. There are a number of reasons for this.

- Muslims regard their religion as the natural way of life: the way Allah made us and intended us to live. Therefore, Allah himself is seen as the originator of this religion; and Adam, as the first person on earth, is seen as the first Muslim.
- The prophets of Islam go right back to Adam. The great prophet Ibrahim (Abraham) for example, who lived about 2500 years before Muhammad, is called a 'Muslim' in the Qur'an (3:60). Remember that a 'Muslim' is someone who 'submits' to the One God; and Jewish, Christian and Islamic traditions all tell of him rejecting polytheism in order to worship the One God. Jews claim to have come from Ibrahim through his son Isaac, and Arabs claim to have come from him through his son Isma'il.

Maulid ul Nabi

The Prophet's Birthday is commemorated on 12 Rabi ul Awwal, and the whole of this third

This is the national flag of Saudi Arabia. It has the declaration of Islamic faith written on it. Try to say it in Arabic *La ilaha illallahu Muhammad-ur-Rasulallah.*

month of the Islamic calendar is special because of it. He is said to have died on the same date, 63 years later.

Maulid ul Nabi is sometimes celebrated with a procession through the streets and a communal meal at the mosque. It is a chance for Muslims to listen to a sermon about Muhammad, to retell stories about him to their children, and to ask Allah 'to kindle in us even a spark of that which motivated and impelled him' (in the words of a Friday sermon, close to Maulid ul Nabi).

Despite Muhammad's importance, Muslims are discouraged from making too much of these celebrations, for the following reasons:

- Maulid ul Nabi was not celebrated for the first four centuries of Islam.
- It is feared that rightful respect for Muhammad could turn into worship of him, which would be idolatry. He was, after all, only human; Islam teaches that Allah alone is to be worshipped. For this reason Muslims have never called Islam 'Muhammadanism'.
- Muslims remember Muhammad *every* day: when they hear the call to prayer; when they ask Allah's blessing upon him during salah; and in trying to follow the Prophet's example in every aspect of their lives.

Maulid ul Nabi celebrations in Mombasa, Kenya.

Activities

Key Elements

1 How are Muslims reminded of the Prophet Muhammad in their call to prayer (see p. 13)? Quote the relevant lines.
2 Why do Muslims show Muhammad so much respect?
3 Why would it be wrong to call Muslims 'Muhammadans'?
4 In what sense is Adam regarded as a Muslim?
5 Why does the Qur'an call Ibrahim a Muslim?

Think About It

6 Islam teaches that we are all born as Muslims. How does this make you feel?
7 Muhammad is seen as the perfect Muslim. He is the ideal that all Muslims try to follow. How important do you think it is to have a figure to look up to and to try to be like?

Muhammad's Early Life

Muhammad was born in Makkah in Arabia, over 1400 years ago (about 570 CE). Makkah was the centre of the economic and religious life of western Arabia, situated as it was on the junction of the main trade routes between Yemen in the southern tip of Arabia, and Syria and Iraq to the north of Arabia. Muhammad was born into the Hashimite family, which was part of the powerful Quraish tribe, whose headquarters were in Makkah.

Like many Arabs from Makkah, his father 'Abdullah made his living by trading; it was on his travels that he was taken ill and died in the city of Yathrib only a few months before Muhammad was born. Muhammad, too, was to work as a trader, leading camel caravans across the deserts. And like his father, was also to die and be buried in Yathrib (which became Madinah).

Tradition tells that the baby Muhammad was sent to a wet-nurse in the desert, according to custom, to benefit from the pure desert air. On returning to the crowded city of Makkah, he had only a few years with his mother, Amina, because she died when Muhammad was six years old. His grandfather, 'Abdul Muttalib, then took charge of him. He was an important leader in Makkah, and is said to have taken the young boy with him to meetings held in the shade of the Ka'bah.

The old man had only a few more years to live, leaving Muhammad in the care of his son, Muhammad's uncle, Abu Talib. He was to give the orphan love and protection, even in later years when Muhammad made many enemies in Makkah. As he grew up, Muhammad sometimes looked after his uncle's sheep. Sometimes he went with his uncle on trading expeditions.

A number of stories surround Muhammad in this period of his life. One tells how he and his uncle stopped at a Christian monastery on their travels, and a monk named Bahira recognised the mark of a prophet on Muhammad's shoulder. Such stories suggest that Allah was preparing Muhammad, in these early years, for his future work.

As a young man, Muhammad showed his concern for justice by becoming a founder-member of a league to protect the safety and rights of strangers in Makkah. He also earned the reputation of being an honest and reliable businessman, and was called **al-Amin**, 'the Trustworthy'. He was too poor to own his own camel caravan, but he so impressed Khadijah, the rich widow for whom he worked, that she proposed to him. Despite the age gap (she was 40 years old, and Muhammad 25), they had a very happy marriage. Although polygamy was practised, Muhammad took no other wife while Khadijah was alive.

Arabian Religion

Makkah was not only a thriving trading centre, but also a holy city. Once a year, the Arab tribesmen converged on Makkah for a pilgrimage. They came to worship and sacrifice animals to the many idols there, which represented their gods and goddesses. In Makkah, three goddesses were given particular honour: Al-Lat the sun-goddess; Al-Uzza the goddess of the planet Venus; and Manat the goddess of good luck. Allah was also worshipped. His name means 'The God', suggesting that he was the supreme, Creator

Activities

Key Elements

1 Copy out this profile of Muhammad and fill in the details:
   Name
   Year of birth
   Tribe
   Father's name
   Mother's name
   Guardian's name (i.e. his uncle)
   Country of origin
   Place of birth
   Place of burial
2 What was Muhammad's nickname and why was he given it?
3 When Muhammad grew up, he showed particular care for widows, orphans and the needy. Why is this understandable, considering his own background?

The Black Stone embedded in the wall of the Ka'bah.

God; but it seems that he had been eclipsed for most Arabs at that time by their many tribal gods.

Of particular interest in Makkah was the Ka'bah, a cube-shaped building which housed some of their 365 idols. It had a stone embedded in its wall, which the Arabs considered to be sacred. The Quraish tribe had custody of the sacred Ka'bah.

Muhammad, like some other Arabs at that time who were called **Hanifs**, became a monotheist, believing that there was only one

God, Allah. He rejected the minor gods and goddesses represented by the idols; nor would he worship the spirits which were believed to haunt natural places like springs, trees, mountains and the winds. (These were called **jinn**, which is where our word 'genie' comes from.) Muhammad could have been influenced in his beliefs by the religions of Judaism and Christianity, which also teach that there is only one God. He would have

Cave Hira on the Mountain of Light.

come across these religions on his travels outside Arabia. There were also some Arab tribes which had converted to Judaism, and there were a few scattered Christian monasteries and holy men in Arabia, seeking the peace and seclusion of the desert.

Muhammad's Call to Prophethood

Muhammad was a thoughtful man and sometimes spent whole nights in prayer. He liked to be alone and would go to the Cave Hira on a mountain five kilometres from Makkah, called Jabal al-Nur, which means 'Mountain of Light'.

One night, when he was 40 years old, he had a religious experience which changed his whole life and the history of the world. He claimed to have seen a vision of a huge figure, which was later identified as Jibreel (the archangel Gabriel). The angel commanded him to read or recite (the Arabic word has both meanings). Since he was illiterate, he kept protesting that he could not read, until finally, in great agitation, he realised that he must *recite* what the angel told him.

This was the first of many such experiences which continued to the end of his life. This is how Islam got its holy book, the Qur'an (which means 'Recitation') as Muhammad passed on the words which he believed had come from Allah. The opening of Chapter 96 of the Qur'an records the first words which were given.

The Blood-Clot

In the Name of God, the Merciful, the Compassionate

Recite: In the Name of thy Lord who created,
*   created Man of a blood-clot.*

Recite: And thy Lord is the Most Generous,
*   who taught by the Pen,*
*   taught Man, that he knew not.*

(Arberry)   *(Qur'an 96:1–5)*

Laylat-ul-Qadr

The Night of Power (**Laylat-ul-Qadr**) is an annual commemoration of that first night when Muhammad began to receive revelations of the Qur'an. This brief chapter of the Qur'an describes that first Night of Power:

Power

In the Name of God, the Merciful, the Compassionate

Behold, We sent it down on the Night of Power;
And what shall teach thee what is the Night of Power?
The Night of Power is better than a thousand months;
*   in it the angels and the Spirit descend,*
by the leave of their Lord, upon every command.
*   Peace it is, till the rising of dawn.*

(Arberry)   *(Qur'an 97)*

This first Night of Power is thought to have occurred during the last ten nights of the month of Ramadan, on an odd number. Most Muslims celebrate it on the night of 27 Ramadan. Many spend the whole night in the mosque, reading the Qur'an and offering prayers. It is said that their prayers will be answered on that night. Some Muslims stay at the mosque for the full ten days, devoting this time to prayer, study of Islam and reading the Qur'an.

Muhammad's Early Prophethood in Makkah

That first terrifying experience in Cave Hira left Muhammad wondering if the words he heard were really from Allah, or if he was going mad. On returning home, he confided in his wife, Khadijah, who reassured him. She consulted her cousin, Waraqah, who was a Christian. He told Muhammad that he was a Messenger from God. Others who knew Muhammad well also believed in him: his cousin, 'Ali; their adopted slave, Zaid; and Abu Bakr, his best friend. In the first few years he made about 50 converts among friends and family.

Then Muhammad began to preach in public, passing on the words that he claimed to have received from Allah. The short chapters of the Qur'an, towards the end of the holy book, are typical of this early period. They denounce idolaters and call on them to worship the One God. Over the next few years his following grew, but so too did the opposition. In 615 CE Muhammad sent some of the Muslims into Christian Ethiopia, to escape persecution. The Year of Mourning, 619, was when his beloved wife died, and also his uncle Abu Talib who, although not a Muslim himself, had given Muhammad the family's protection. This was now withdrawn.

Isra' wal Mi'raj

This commemorates the Night Journey and Ascension, an experience Muhammad had about this time, when he most needed reassurance. It is claimed that in one night he travelled all the way from the Holy Mosque in Makkah to the 'Further Mosque' of Jerusalem. Tradition tells that this miraculous journey was on a winged horse called Buraq, and that Muhammad ascended into heaven from the famous rock in Jerusalem over which the Dome of the Rock now stands. There he spoke to the prophets of old and brought back the command to pray to Allah five times a day.

Isra' wal Mi'raj is remembered each year on 27 Rajab. It is celebrated by reading the Qur'an (particularly Chapter 17, 'The Night Journey') and by saying extra prayers that night.

The Dome of the Rock. A mosque was first built here by Caliph 'Umar in 638 CE. This beautiful building dates from 687 CE. It covers the huge rock from which Muhammad is believed to have ascended to heaven. The Dome of the Rock is more a shrine than a mosque, and another mosque was built nearby, soon afterwards, with much more room inside for Muslims to gather for prayer. That one is called the Al-Aksa Mosque, meaning 'The Further Mosque', to commemorate the miraculous Night Journey.

Activities

Key Elements

1 What is polytheism? (Look it up in a dictionary if necessary.)
2 What word describes belief in one God?
3 Name the two great monotheistic religions which existed in Muhammad's time.
4 Why is it suggested that Muhammad was influenced by Judaism and/or Christianity?
5 Why do Muslims like to visit Cave Hira in Arabia?
6 What was the main message that Muhammad preached?

Think About It

7 Why do you think Muhammad took no other wife while Khadijah lived?
8 Do you think it was easier for Muhammad's friends and family to believe that he was a prophet, than for strangers to believe in him?
9 What do you think really happened on **Isra' wal Mi'raj**?

The Hijrah

Matters came to a head in 622 CE when there was a serious plot to assassinate Muhammad. By this time his influence had spread 480 km beyond Makkah, to the city of Yathrib. A number of its citizens had been converted to Islam when visiting Makkah on pilgrimage, and they now invited Muhammad to become their leader, hoping he could settle some internal squabbles.

Having put up with hardship and persecution for many years now, Muhammad obviously felt that it was the will of Allah for him to leave Makkah. So, on 16 July 622, Muhammad set out by night with Abu Bakr, on the journey to Yathrib. This is known as the **Hijrah**, the Arabic word for 'emigration'. Muhammad had already sent on ahead of him over a hundred Muslim families; and more joined them from Ethiopia. The Muslims had the following titles:

- **The Companions** were all those Muslims who knew Muhammad in his lifetime;
- **The Emigrants** were all those who had come with him to Yathrib;
- **The Helpers** were citizens of Yathrib who had converted to Islam.

Later, Yathrib was called **al-Madinah**, in Muhammad's honour – 'the Town' (of the Prophet). It was the first Islamic city-state.

1st Muharram

So important was the Hijrah, as the start of the time when a community was first run on Islamic lines, that it became the beginning of the Muslim calendar. Islamic years are dated AH (from the Latin *anno Hegirae* – 'in the year of the Hijrah'). So 622 CE became 1 AH for the Muslims.

Muharram is the first month in the Islamic calendar, so 1st Muharram is New Year's Day. This commemorates the Hijrah but, like the remembrance of the Prophet's Birthday, it is not seen as an opportunity for wild celebrations, but for remembering the life and example of Muhammad. Muslims attend mosque

The Islamic calendar

	Months (29/30 days)		Commemorations
1	Muharram	1st	The Day of Hijrah; New Year
2	Safar		
3	Rabi ul Awwal	12th	Maulid ul Nabi (Birthday of the Prophet)
4	Rabi ul Akhir		
5	Jamada al Awwal		
6	Jamada al Akhir		
7	Rajab	27th	Isra' wal Mi'raj (Night Journey and Ascension)
8	Sha'ban		
9	Ramadan	27th	Laylat-ul-Qadr (Night of Power)
10	Shawwal	1st	Id-ul-Fitr (Minor Festival)
11	Dhul Qi'da		
12	Dhul-Hijjah	10th	Id-ul-Adha (Major Festival)

for special prayers and a sermon about Muhammad's career, especially the event of the Hijrah. Just as Muhammad left behind his enemies in Makkah, so Muslims are encouraged to leave behind them all that is bad in their lives and to try to be better Muslims.

The Period in Madinah

Almost half Muhammad's years of prophethood were spent in Madinah, where he proved himself a very capable leader. He ruled from a simple home which he had helped build and which was adjacent to the first mosque. In Makkah he had preached a basic message of belief in Allah, the One God; that he was Allah's messenger; and that the Day of Judgement was coming. Now, with the establishment of the first Islamic state, the religion became more organised, with detailed instructions about prayer, fasting, charity and pilgrimage. He was also asked for advice on how to behave in all spheres of life, such as work, leisure and family relations, and he answered either with quotations from the Qur'an or with sayings of his own.

Unfortunately, hostility continued between Makkah and Madinah, and two significant battles were fought. In 624 the Muslims, although outnumbered, won a resounding victory at the Battle of Badr. But in the following year, they lost the Battle of Uhud against a massive army from Makkah. In 627 the Makkans besieged Madinah; but the city survived, due largely to the digging of a trench around it. Finally a truce was agreed, the Hudaybiya peace treaty, which allowed Muslims to visit the holy city of Makkah on pilgrimage. By 630, the treaty having been broken by the Makkans, the Muslims were strong enough to advance on Makkah with a huge army of 20 000 men. There was no resistance. Muhammad generously spared his enemies, but insisted that the idols of Makkah be destroyed. He had reclaimed the holy city for Allah.

Muhammad's Wives

It is thought that Muhammad took 12 wives in all, during his time at Madinah. Remember that polygamy was perfectly acceptable in Arabia at that time. Many of his new wives were the widows of his followers who had been killed in battle and who now had no one to protect them. Other wives came through marriage alliances as Muhammad extended his influence over more and more Arab tribes. Ayesha, the daughter of his closest friend, Abu Bakr, was the only one who had not been married before. When Muhammad had been married to Khadijah his first wife, he had taken no others. They had had six or seven children (although only his four daughters had grown up). Now, in Madinah, with his many wives, only one more child was born to Muhammad.

The Farewell Pilgrimage

In March 632, Muhammad went on pilgrimage to Makkah for the last time, and delivered his famous Farewell Speech to his fellow pilgrims. It began:

> 'O People, lend me an attentive ear, for I know not whether, after this year, I shall ever be amongst you again. Therefore listen to what I am saying to you very carefully and take these words to those who could not be present here today.'

Most of the sermon concerns human rights, and Muhammad also enforced the five essential practices of Islam, known as the Five Pillars:

> 'O People, listen to me in earnest, worship Allah, say your five daily prayers (Salah), fast during the month of Ramadan, and give your wealth in Zakat. Perform Hajj if you can afford to.'

He finished with these words:

> 'O People, no prophet or apostle will come after me and no new faith will be born. Reason well, therefore, O People, and under-

The Prophet's Mosque at Madinah, illuminated by night.

stand my words which I convey to you. I leave behind me two things, the Qur'an and my example the Sunnah and if you follow these you will never go astray.

'All those who listen to me shall pass on my words to others and those to others again; and may the last ones understand my words better than those who listen to me directly. Be my witness, O Allah, that I have conveyed your message to your people.'

(*From* The Prophet Muhammad's Last Sermon)

A few months later, Muhammad died of fever and was buried in Madinah. His tomb is still there, under the green dome of the Prophet's Mosque, with those of his two successors, Abu Bakr and 'Umar.

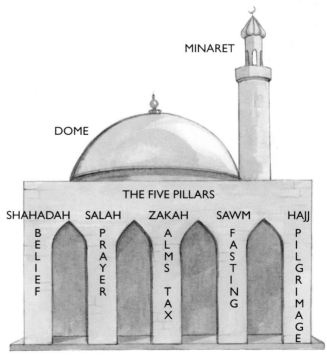

MINARET

DOME

THE FIVE PILLARS

SHAHADAH SALAH ZAKAH SAWM HAJJ

BELIEF PRAYER ALMS TAX FASTING PILGRIMAGE

Activities

Key Elements

1 Where did Muhammad and his followers settle after leaving Makkah?
2 Explain why the Islamic dating system uses the letters AH.
3 What are the names of the two famous battles that Muhammad fought while living at Madinah (the first of which he won, and the second he lost)?
4 Why did Muhammad marry more wives in Madinah?
5 When did Muhammad deliver his Farewell Speech?

Think About It

6 Why do you think Muhammad's Farewell Speech is given such importance in Islam?
7 Why do you think the five main obligatory duties for Muslims are called the Five Pillars?

Jihad – Holy War

While they lived in Makkah, the Muslims refused to fight against their enemies, even though they were provoked. But eventually, in Madinah, Muhammad came to believe that war is sometimes right and that to fight in defence of Islam is to fight for Allah.

The first big battle, the Battle of Badr, was fought with just over 300 men and boys against a Makkan force of 1000. The Muslim victory was seen as proof that their religion was right, for Allah was obviously on their side. The Muslims must have felt like David the shepherd-boy who fought for the Lord's people against the giant, Goliath. David is regarded as a prophet, in Islam, and his victory is referred to in the Qur'an.

So they routed them by Allah's leave and David slew Goliath; and Allah gave him the kingdom and wisdom, and taught him of that which He willeth. And if Allah had not repelled some men by others the earth would have been corrupted. But Allah is a Lord of Kindness to (his) creatures.

(Pickthall) *(Qur'an 2:251)*

A Muslim commentary on this text says this:

The essential point is that we must fight for the preservation of our Faith, no matter how overwhelming the odds may seem. In fact, if we fight for Allah with courage and unshakeable belief it is our foes who face overwhelming odds, for Allah has promised He will aid us.

(The Essential Teaching of Islam, p. 161)

Islam calls war which is fought for Allah **jihad**, or 'holy war'. The Qur'an teaches that it should only be fought by Muslims in self-defence, or in defence of Islam. It should not be used to try to convert people to Islam, and it should be stopped when the enemy wants peace. Muhammad made further regulations, forbidding civilian casualties. He also set an example of mercy to the conquered. Islam teaches that those who die fighting in holy war will go straight to heaven. This has been a powerful incentive to Muslim soldiers, and an important factor in the success of many Islamic wars.

Chapter 2 of the Qur'an makes a number of points about jihad:

Warfare is ordained for you, though it is hateful unto you; but it may happen that ye hate a thing which is good for you, and it may happen that ye love a thing which is bad for you. Allah knoweth, ye know not.

(Pickthall)   *(Qur'an 2:216)*

Fight in the way of Allah against those who fight against you, but begin not hostilities. Lo! Allah loveth not aggressors.

(Pickthall)   *(Qur'an 2:190)*

But if they desist, then lo! Allah is Forgiving, Merciful. And fight them until persecution is no more, and religion is for Allah. But if they desist, then let there be no hostility except against wrongdoers.

(Pickthall)   *(Qur'an 2:192–3)*

Throughout the ages, there have been occasions when some Muslims have been called to take up arms for their faith. But for all Muslims there is the greater holy war. The word *jihad* literally means 'striving', and it also describes the effort that Muslims must make to do Allah's will every day of their lives. It means fighting all the evil thoughts and desires within ourselves, like greed, envy, lust and laziness. It means being prepared to do something about the injustices we see all around us, like defending the weak against the bullies, sending money to the starving people in developing countries, speaking out about cruelty to animals or wastage of the world's resources. Jihad demands sacrifice – sacrifice of one's time, skills, money, even perhaps of one's life.

Jihad is so important that some Muslims regard it as the Sixth Pillar of Islam.

Activities

Key Elements

1 When can war be regarded as 'holy' in Islam?

Think About It

2 Do you think war can ever be 'holy'?
3 Why do you think striving against our own faults is regarded as the *greater* holy war?

Vocabulary

Give the Arabic words for the following:

1 the Prophet's Birthday
2 'The Trustworthy'
3 'The God'
4 spirits
5 'one who is inclined' to believe in one God
6 the holy book of Islam
7 the Emigration
8 the Night of Power
9 Night Journey and Ascension
10 striving/holy war

Assignments

1   Arabian Religion

a) Write a short account of Arabian polytheism in Muhammad's time.

b) Give some religious reasons for rejecting polytheism and idolatry.

c) Why do you think the polytheists of Makkah turned against Muhammad?

2   Muhammad's Childhood

a) Find out more about the story of Bahira *or* about another of the miraculous stories surrounding Muhammad's childhood (e.g. his mother's vision; or the opening of his chest by angels to wash his heart). Record the story.

b) Explain what the story is telling us about Muhammad.

c) Do you think the story is true? Does it have any truth in it? Explain your answers.

3   The Night of Power

a) Describe what happened to Muhammad on the Night of Power.

b) Explain as fully as possible why this was such a significant moment in the history of Islam.

c) What was there about the situation which might have led Muhammad to have a religious experience?

4   Muhammad

a) Find out more about the life of Muhammad, and make notes to supplement the information in this chapter, particularly on Muhammad's periods of prophethood in Makkah and Madinah.

b) Make a simple story-book on Muhammad *for Muslim children*.

(Remember not to draw pictures of Muhammad.) You should cover the main points in each period of his life, describing them in such a way that you emphasise their importance for Islam.

c) Assess the importance and influence of Muhammad.

4

Scriptures and Beliefs

The Qur'an

Origin

Muslims believe that the words of the Qur'an come from Allah himself, and were passed on to humanity through the Prophet Muhammad. So they do not regard Muhammad as its author. Instead, he is believed to have recited accurately the words which were revealed to him by the angel Jibreel, who is also said to have told Muhammad the order in which the passages were to go. People who heard Muhammad jotted down these words on all sorts of scraps of writing material, or committed them to memory. They were collected together into a book immediately after Muhammad's death, under the direction of Abu Bakr, his successor. Various copies of the Qur'an circulated in its early years until 'Uthman, the third successor of Muhammad,

Illuminated pages of the Qur'an, in Arabic.

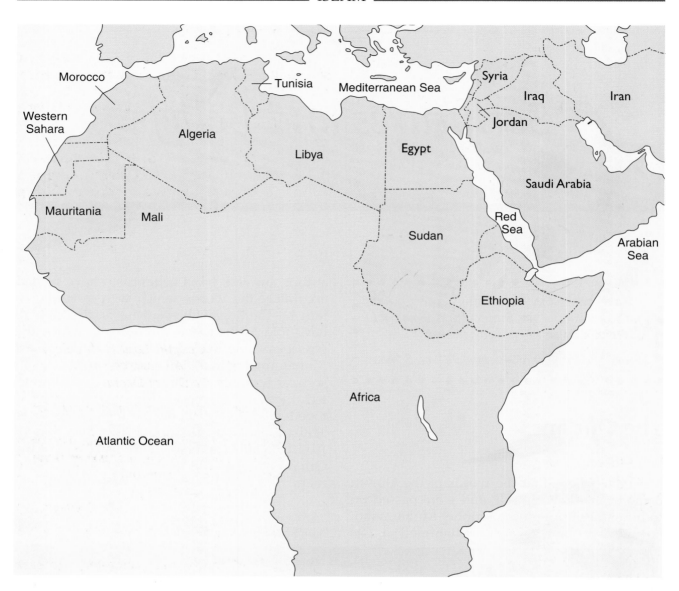

Main areas of Arabic-speaking people.

recalled them and issued standardised copies, based on the original, to the main Islamic cities. All copies since then have been identical.

Language

Since the Qur'an is believed to be from Allah, every word, every letter, is sacred to Muslims. It is therefore considered very important to keep the Qur'an in the language in which it was first spoken, i.e. Arabic. As Islam spread from Arabia, its language was adopted by a number of Islamic countries, and is still spoken in these countries today (as the map shows). Muslims in these countries should find the Qur'an quite easy to read, even

though the style of modern Arabic has naturally changed since Muhammad's time.

In other countries, Muslims need to learn enough Arabic to take part in their worship and to read the Qur'an. You can find translations of the Qur'an for people who do not know Arabic, or copies with both Arabic and another language for those who do not have Arabic as their first language; but Muslims do not accept these translations as proper Qur'ans. They regard them as interpretations rather than the real thing. Translating one language into another must involve an element of interpretation, in trying to choose equivalent words and expressions. For this reason, Islam has insisted that the Qur'an must remain as if it believes it was revealed from Allah. It is too precious to risk losing any of its meaning; apart from which, the very sound of the Arabic Qur'an is sacred to Muslims.

Arabic is written from right to left, and books written in Arabic will open in this direction. So the Qur'an looks as if it starts at the back, to those of us who read books in languages which use the Latin alphabet. In the same way English books look back-to-front to Arabic-speaking people.

As-Salamu-Alaykum, 'Peace be with you'. This is the common Muslim greeting in Arabic.

Style

The Qur'an is written in verses of different lengths held together by loose rhymes. The beauty and majesty of this language is usually lost in translation, but A. J. Arberry's version, *The Koran Interpreted*, tries to retain the rhythmic patterns of the original.

All but one of the chapters (Chapter 9) begin with the words: 'In the name of God, the Merciful, the Compassionate.' This is known as the **Bismillah**, its first word in Arabic: *'Bismillah ir Rahman ir Rahim'*.

Title

The Arabic word *Qur'an* means 'recitation', and it is an appropriate title. Muhammad was commanded to recite the words given him by the angel Jibreel (Gabriel). Muslims recite passages of the Qur'an at their five daily prayer sessions. Children are taught how to recite the Qur'an; you can see them nodding their heads up and down to the rhythm of the words. When someone has learnt the whole Qur'an by heart, he is called a **hafiz** and she is called a **hafizah**.

Length and Layout

The Qur'an has 114 chapters, which are called **surahs**. Muslims tend to know them by their titles rather than their numbers. So, for instance, Chapter 1 is 'The Opening' (*Fatihah* in Arabic); and Chapter 2 is 'The Cow' – named after the story of the yellow cow in verses 67–71. There are over 6000 verses in the Qur'an; but the verse divisions are not always identical, and this can cause problems if you are looking up references.

> 1
> *The Opening*
>
> *In the Name of God, the Merciful, the Compassionate*
>
> *Praise belongs to God, the Lord of all Being,
> the All-merciful, the All-compassionate,
>   the Master of the Day of Doom.*
>
> *Thee only we serve; to Thee alone we pray for succour.*
>
> *Guide us in the straight path, the path of those whom Thou hast blessed, not of those against whom Thou art wrathful,
>   nor of those who are astray.*
>
> (Arberry)

Apart from the opening chapter, those at the beginning of the Qur'an tend to be the longest, with the very short chapters at the end. Chapter 2, for example, is the longest of all the surahs, with 286 verses, many of which are themselves quite long; but the last four surahs have only between four and six lines each. Most of the short chapters come from Muhammad's early period in Makkah, when he was preaching a simple message of belief in the One God and warning of eternal punishment for idolaters. These surahs are short and sharp. The longer chapters belong to Muhammad's period in Madinah, when the Islamic community needed more detailed guidance. M. M. Pickthall's English interpretation, called *The Meaning of the Glorious Koran*, has an index at the back listing the places where each surah was revealed.

Number	Name	Where revealed	Page
I	The Opening	Mecca	31
II	The Cow	Al-Madinah	34
III	The Family in 'Imran	Al-Madinah	62
IV	Women	Al-Madinah	79
V	The Table Spread	Al-Madinah	96
VI	Cattle	Mecca	108
VII	The Heights	Mecca	122
VIII	Spoils of War	Al-Madinah	139
IX	Repentance	Al-Madinah	145
X	Jonah	Mecca	157
XI	Hud	Mecca	165
XII	Joseph	Mecca	174
XIII	The Thunder	Mecca	182
XIV	Abraham	Mecca	186
XV	Al-Hijr	Mecca	191
XVI	The Bee	Mecca	195
XVII	The Children of Israel	Mecca	204
XVIII	The Cave	Mecca	212
XIX	Mary	Mecca	221
XX	Ta Ha	Mecca	228

This is taken from Pickthall's *The Meaning of the Glorious Koran* (p. 456). It accounts for half of the Qur'an, but only the first 20 chapters. What does this tell us about the length of the remaining 94 chapters?

Activities

Key Elements

1 What is the Qur'an?
2 What does the word 'Qur'an' mean and why?
3 Whom do Muslims believe to be the author of the Qur'an?
4 In which language is the Qur'an written?
5 Why is it important for Muslims to read it in this language rather than in a translation, if they speak another language?

6 Why do the longer chapters (**surahs**) belong to the period Muhammad spent in Madinah?
7 Using the chart of surah headings, name someone from the Qur'an who also appears in the Old Testament, and another person who also appears in the New Testament.

Think About It

8 If a holy book is believed to be the 'revealed Word of God', does this necessarily mean that every single word of it is inspired?

9 Give arguments for and against translating a holy book into different languages.

Treatment

Muslims show their respect for the Qur'an by treating it with great care. They wrap each copy in a clean piece of cloth, or in a special cloth bag which is stitched in the shape of an envelope. They keep it on the highest shelf in the room, to show its superiority, and they would never put anything on top of it. They wash before touching it, at the very least their hands, and some Muslims perform full wudu (see pp. 14–15). Girls and women cover their heads with a scarf when reading it and boys and men will usually wear a prayer cap. They do this out of respect. As it is customary for Arabs to sit on the floor, a folding book-stand is used when reading the Qur'an, so that the holy book does not touch the ground. Muslims are not allowed to eat or drink, smoke or talk in the same room where it is being read, for they must give it their full attention. If they have any posters or other wall-hangings with words of the Qur'an on them, they are put on a wall which they face, so that they do not turn their backs on them.

Use

The Qur'an is part of a Muslim's daily life. Muslim men and women recite or read it often; some carry pocket-size editions around with them. The opening chapter of the Qur'an is recited at the beginning of each rak'ah (see pp. 16–17) at the five daily prayers, and it may be followed by any other passage from the Qur'an. The Qur'an is divided into 30 sections, one for each day, to make it easy to recite it right through during a month. Muslims try to do this especially during the holy month of Ramadan. It is also recited at all special religious celebrations.

Importance

Muslims believe that the Qur'an is a perfect copy of a heavenly book, and that it is the last revelation of Allah's truth to the human world. They believe that it is therefore the best guide we can have in living our lives as Allah intended, and that this is the way to salvation.

A book which trains young Muslim chil-

That is the Book, wherein is no doubt, a guidance to the godfearing.

(Arberry)   *(Qur'an 2:2)*

Today I have perfected your religion for you, and I have completed My blessing upon you, and I have approved Islam for your religion.

(Arberry)   *(Qur'an 5:5)*

dren in their faith sums up the importance of the Qur'an like this:

It is the Last and Final Book sent by God.
The Quran is a Great Book.
Its style is beautiful.
Its language is sweet.
Its message is full of life.
It tells us how to worship God.
It tells us how to live a life of virtue.

– – –

A Muslim believes in the Quran.
A Muslim reads the Quran.
A Muslim tries to follow the Quran.
          (From First Primer of Islam)

In the following quotation, a Muslim explains the importance of the Qur'an.

The Qur'an is an old book and the translations into English leave much to be desired. It is not written down in any logical order and there is much apparent repetition. It is like a goldmine with nuggets of wisdom waiting at every turn to be discovered and treasured – and the gold is as bright today as it was fourteen centuries ago.

All that we struggle for today was also the struggle, the jihad, *then. Justice, compassion for the weak and oppressed, women's rights, equitable distribution of property, concern for the environment and the sanctity of life.*

Even its penal code, much maligned of late as barbaric, makes provision for offenders to be encouraged to ask forgiveness and gives them several opportunities to change their ways before the ultimate penalties are imposed. It bears a resemblance to some of the more humane societies of today which try to re-educate offenders to a sense of their social responsibilities.

The vision of the Qur'an is based upon a clear decision to believe in God. And it invites others to make that decision, promising great spiritual rewards....

Muhammad was under no illusion that everyone would agree with him or accept what he said. Nor did he try to force anyone to agree. But such was the power of his vision that it did eventually succeed in capturing the imaginations of even his worst enemies. It still continues to inspire many young (and old) reformers today as well as influencing the day-to-day lives of Muslims everywhere.

(Harfiyah Ball *in* New Internationalist)

Further Information
Surah 2

Pickthall argues that Chapter 2 was revealed during the first four years after the Hijrah, and most of it within the first 18 months, before the Battle of Badr. This is because much of it concerns the relationship between Islam and Judaism, which was an important issue when Muhammad arrived in Madinah; the Jewish tribes there welcomed him at first but then turned against him. Also, there are instructions about holy war, which was necessary for the first time at the Battle of Badr. Prior to this the Muslims had practised non-violence. This is how Pickthall concludes his introduction to Chapter 2:

This surah might be described as the Koran in little. It contains mention of all the essential points of the Revelation, which are elaborated elsewhere. This accounts for the precedence given to it in the arrangement of the Book.

The period of revelation is the years 1 and 2 AH for the most part, certain verses of legislation being considered as of later date.

(p. 34)

Hadith

Muslims first of all turn to the Qur'an for guidance, but they also have the Hadith. The word hadith means a 'statement' or 'report'; and the books of Hadith are collections of reports of what Muhammad said, did or approved in particular situations. Some **ahadith** (plural) are especially important because they record the **sunnah** of Muhammad, i.e. his 'custom', 'practice' or 'way' (of doing things), which he wanted Muslims to follow. So, apart from the rules in the Qur'an, Muslims also have the example of Muhammad himself, showing how the Prophet put the Qur'anic rules and ideals into practice. The precise times of the five daily prayers, for example, are laid down in the Hadith, but are not made clear in the Qur'an. The Qur'an itself says: 'You have had a good example in God's Messenger.' (33:21).

Notice that there is a firm distinction made between what Muhammad said when he claimed to be passing on revelations which had come to him from Allah, which form the Qur'an, and when he was giving his own teaching which is recorded in the Hadith.

Each Hadith records both the information about Muhammad and its chain of transmission, for example, 'X reported that Y reported that Z reported that 'Uthman reported that the Messenger of Allah (Pbuh) said . . .' The chain is not usually quoted today, only the text: 'Uthman reported that the Messenger of Allah (peace and blessings of Allah be upon him) said: The best amongst you is the person who learnt Al-Qur'an and taught it.' (Bukhari; *Selection from Hadith*, No. 102, p. 55.)

Most Muslims accept six books of Hadith as being the most trustworthy. These are known as The Accurate Six and were collected within the first three centuries of Islam. The two most authoritative books are called **sahih**, meaning 'sound'; they are Sahih Al-Bukhari and Sahih Muslim.

Activities

Key Elements

1 Name two things Muslims do to show respect for their copies of the Qur'an.
2 Which is the most frequently quoted chapter (surah) of the Qur'an?
3 What is a hadith?
4 Name one of the compilers of the Hadith.
5 Why is it important for Muslims to know the sunnah of the Prophet as well as the Qur'an?

Think About It

6 What difference do you think it would make to you if you spent time each day reciting and thinking about verses from a holy book?
7 'The Qur'an is an ancient book which cannot help us in our modern world.' How do you think a Muslim would answer this?

The Five Articles of Faith

The following verse from the Qur'an sums up the Five Articles of Faith (**iman**) in Islam, which it says have been revealed or 'sent down' from Allah. It speaks of belief in:

- God (Allah)
- His angels
- His books
- His Messengers (the Prophets)
- 'The homecoming' (life after death)

The Messenger believes in what was sent down to him from his Lord, and the believers; each one believes in God and His angels, and in His Books and His Messengers; we make no division between any one of His Messengers. They say, 'We hear, and obey. Our Lord, grant us Thy forgiveness; unto Thee is the homecoming.'

(Arberry) *(Qur'an 2:285)*

1 Belief in Allah

The first Article of Faith is the same as the first Pillar of Faith: belief in Allah, the One God (Allah means 'The God'). The first Pillar can be called both the **Shahadah** and the **Kalimah**. Shahadah comes from the Arabic *ash-hadu*, meaning 'I declare'; and it describes a profession of faith. Kalimah is the term used for a statement of faith. (Strictly speaking, there are two kalimahs in the declaration that: 'There is no god but Allah, and Muhammad is the Messenger of Allah.')

The first Article of Faith is belief in **tawhid**, which means the oneness and unity of Allah. If there is only one God, then he alone is the creator of all that exists, but was not himself created, he is 'The Eternal'. If there is only one God, then he alone is in control of the universe, he is 'The Almighty', 'The Omnipotent'.

Tawhid has some far-reaching implications in Islam.

- Muslims should worship Allah alone; no one else and nothing else is worthy. No other being should be associated with Allah. Idolatry is worshipping something less than God, and it is strictly forbidden. This sin of idolatry is called **shirk**, and is regarded by Muslims as the worst of all sins.
- Although Muslims are held responsible for their own sins, they also believe that nothing happens unless it is the will of Allah. They frequently say *'Insha Allah'*, meaning 'If Allah is willing', showing their recognition of his power and acceptance of his will for them.
- A Muslim's whole life should be lived for Allah alone. Islam gives rules to govern all aspects of one's life.
- If there is only one God, there should be only one religion. Islam is seen as the best religion for the whole world.
- Those who believe in the oneness of Allah should be united together in their religion. Islam emphasises the unity of the **Ummah**, the world-wide Islamic community.
- Belief in one creator gives a sense of oneness with all creation. Therefore Muslims should respect other human beings, animals and natural resources.

Further Information
Further Implications of Tawhid

- Muslims are conscious of Allah looking over them at all times, knowing what they are thinking and doing. This should make them more likely to do right.

- Muslims should be modest because they recognise that there is a far greater power than that of human beings, and they know that they must submit to Allah, on whom they depend utterly.
- On the other hand, they must submit *only* to Allah. So Muslims should not be overawed by other people or by human inventions.
- They should be confident, because they trust in Allah and believe that nothing can happen unless he wills it. Life and death are entirely in his hands.
- They should be contented, because they believe that power, wealth and success come from Allah alone, and he gives them to whom he wants. Muslims should live honest lives, doing their best and accepting what Allah gives them, but without being envious of others or too ambitious.

Allahu Akbar (The Takbir), 'Allah is the Greatest'.

Some of the 99 Beautiful Names

These describe Allah's qualities, and are found in the Qur'an (Ar, Al, As and An mean 'The').

Ar-Rahman	The Merciful
Ar-Rahīm	The Compassionate
Al-Malik	The One Who Rules
As-Salām	The Peace
Al-'Azīz	The Almighty/Powerful
Al-Khāliq	The Creator
Al-Hakam	The Judge
Al-Halīm	The Patient
Al-Karīm	The Generous
Al-Mujīb	The One Who Answers
Al-Mumīt	The Bringer of Death
As-Samad	The Perfect/Eternal
An-Nūr	The Light
Ar-Rashīd	The Guide

2 Belief in Angels

Islam teaches that Allah is the only spiritual being to be worshipped, but that there are other supernatural beings, said to be created from light, called angels. These are the heavenly servants of Allah. Unlike human beings, the angels have no free will of their own, and are therefore sinless.

Muhammad said these angels surround us at all times and will present a full report on us after death. It is believed that two angels come to the grave to take charge of the soul until the Day of Resurrection.

In the following verses of the Qur'an, the two archangels, Gabriel (Jibreel) and Michael are named. Gabriel is also referred to in the Qur'an as the holy spirit (which must not be confused with the Christian idea of God, the

Say (O Muhammad, to mankind): Who is an enemy to Gabriel! For he it is who hath revealed (this Scripture) to thy heart by Allah's leave, confirming that which was (revealed) before it, and a guidance and glad tidings to believers;

Who is an enemy to Allah, and His angels and His messengers, and Gabriel and Michael! Then, lo! Allah (Himself) is an enemy to the disbelievers.

(Pickthall)   *(Qur'an 2:97–98)*

Holy Spirit). Islam teaches that Gabriel brought Allah's revelations to the Prophets and, in particular, the Qur'an to Muhammad.

Another, Izrail, the 'angel of death', will blow the trumpet to herald the Last Day. We also read of Iblis, the fallen angel. This is Islam's name for the Devil or Satan. In the creation story, we read this:

And when We said unto the angels: Prostrate yourselves before Adam, they fell prostrate, all save Iblis. He demurred through pride, and so became a disbeliever.

(Pickthall)   *(Qur'an 2:34)*

(Note that 'We' refers to Allah. Like the 'royal we', it refers to only one person.)

3 Belief in Holy Books

Muslims believe that, through the ages, Allah has revealed his truth through his prophets, and that this has been written down in holy books. They believe that Ibrahim brought a book, which is now lost. They accept the Jewish Scriptures: the Tawrah brought by Musa (the Torah of Moses), and the Zabur of Dawud (the Psalms of David). They also believe in the Injil of 'Isa (the Gospel brought by Jesus). They believe that Allah sent other holy books to other people of the world, which are not named in the Qur'an.

Muslims believe that most of these revelations are now lost. The others they consider to be corrupted, i.e. Allah's words became mixed up with human interpretations, and there is now no means of knowing what is true. Therefore, although they believe that Allah inspired both Judaism and Christianity, they do not accept everything that their Scriptures say. Muslims also believe that Allah sent books at certain times in history to particular people. So his rules for the Jews, for example, do not necessarily apply to all people for all time.

So it was necessary for Allah to send down a further revelation: the Holy Qur'an. Islam teaches that this book contains the complete and uncorrupted words of Allah for all people, everywhere, in all ages. They believe the Qur'an is the timeless truth from Allah to humanity.

> *Allah hath revealed the Scripture with the truth.*
>
> (Qur'an 2:176)
>
> *Those unto whom We have given the Scripture, who read it with the right reading, those believe in it. And whoso disbelieveth in it, those are they who are the losers.*
>
> (Pickthall)   (Qur'an 2:121)

4   Belief in Prophethood

> *Say (O Muslims): We believe in Allah and that which is revealed unto us and that which was revealed unto Abraham, and Ishmael, and Isaac, and Jacob, and the tribes, and that which Moses and Jesus received, and that which the Prophets received from their Lord.*
>
> (Pickthall)   (Qur'an 2:136)

A prophet is someone through whom Allah speaks. The Qur'an names 25 prophets (most of whom are found in the Bible); but tradition says there have been 124 000 in all. **Nabi** is the word used for most of these prophets; but **rasul** describes a prophet who has brought a holy book. These are known as the Messengers of Allah. So, belief in prophethood is closely linked with the third Article of Faith: belief in holy books.

Islam teaches that, since all true prophets were inspired by Allah, they all brought the same basic truth: that there is only one God, and that he will punish the wicked and reward the good. Some people believed these prophets, but there were always those who rejected them, and their messages were lost or distorted.

For Muslims, Muhammad is Allah's last prophet, known as the 'Seal of the Prophets' (33:40), who brought the final message which has been preserved intact in the Qur'an. This

is the final and complete message from Allah to humanity. Muslims therefore strongly deny any claims to prophethood that have been made since the time of Muhammad.

The Prophets of Islam

Whenever Muslims mention a prophet, they say 'Peace be upon him' (Pbuh).

Here are the names of the prophets of Islam.

Qur'anic name	Biblical name
Adam	Adam
Idrīs	Enoch
Nūh	Noah
Hūd	
Sālih	
Ibrāhīm	Abraham
Ismā'īl	Ishmael
Ishāq	Isaac
Lūt	Lot
Ya'qūb	Jacob
Yūsuf	Joseph
Shu'ayb	
Ayyūb	Job
Mūsa	Moses
Hārūn	Aaron
Dhu'l-kifl	Ezekiel
Dawūd	David
Sulaymān	Solomon
Iliās	Elias/Elijah
Al-Yasa'	Elisha
Yunūs	Jonah
Zakariyya	Zechariah
Yahya	John
'Isa	Jesus
Muhammad	

5   Belief in Life after Death

Belief in life after death (**akhirah**) is fundamental to Islam. The Qur'an is full of warnings to disbelievers about the doom awaiting them after death, as well as of promises of good things for those who submit to Allah. The Hadith, too, contain much teaching on this important matter.

Muslims believe that this life is only a short part of our existence. This is our chance to live good lives, as Allah intended, or to turn our backs on Allah and his laws. They believe that after death we shall have to answer for the way we have used our lives, and this will affect our eternal destinies.

Muhammad taught that, at death, souls are questioned by two angels who ask: 'Who is your Lord?' 'What is your religion?' and 'Who is that man who was sent amongst you?', i.e. the Prophet (*Selection from Hadith*, p. 176). Those who know that Allah is the only God and that Muhammad is his Prophet, remain in comfort until the Day of Resurrection. The rest are kept in great discomfort.

> 'Uthman reported that when the Holy Prophet (peace and blessings of Allah be upon him) had completed the burial of the dead he stood on his grave and said: Seek forgiveness for your brother and beseech (Allah) for his steadfastness (in the hour of his trial) for now he is being questioned.
>
> (Abu Dawud; Selection from Hadith, No. 340, p. 175)

Islam teaches that, at the Last Day, the end of the world will come. Then everyone will be raised up and each individual will be judged by Allah himself. Everyone will be sorry – for the wrong they have done, and for not doing more good with their lives. People will be judged not only on their deeds but also on

> The unbelievers of the People of the Book and the idolaters shall be in the Fire of Gehenna,
>   therein dwelling forever;
>   those are the worst of creatures.
> But those who believe, and do righteous deeds,
>   those are the best of creatures;
>   their recompense is with their Lord –
> Gardens of Eden, underneath which rivers flow,
>   therein dwelling for ever and ever.
> God is well-pleased with them, and they are well-pleased with Him;
>   that is for him who fears his Lord.
>
> (Arberry)   (Qur'an 98:5–8)

their faith. Believers will have their sins forgiven and will go to heaven, for Allah is merciful and compassionate; but disbelievers will go to hell. They had their chance on earth to turn to Allah, and now it is too late. Heaven and hell are described in the Qur'an as physical states: the one, like a wonderful garden, where people will be young again and able to enjoy all its pleasures; the other, like a scorching fire that is never put out.

> *The Splitting*
>
> In the Name of God, the Merciful, the Compassionate.
>   When heaven is split open,
>   when the stars are scattered,
>   when the seas swarm over,
>   when the tombs are overthrown,
> then a soul shall know its works, the former and the latter.
>
> O Man! What deceived thee as to thy generous Lord
> who created thee and shaped thee and wrought thee in symmetry
>   and composed thee after what form He would?
>
>   No indeed; but you cry lies to the Doom;
>   yet there are over you watchers
>   noble, writers
>   who know whatever you do.
>
>   Surely the pious shall be in bliss,
>   and the libertines shall be in a fiery furnace
>   roasting therein on the Day of Doom,
>   nor shall they ever be absent from it.
>
> And what shall teach thee what is the Day of Doom?
> Again, what shall teach thee what is the Day of Doom?
> A day when no soul shall possess aught to succour another soul;
>   that day the Command shall belong unto God.
>
> (Arberry)   (Qur'an 82)

43

The sheer scale of the physical destruction on the Day of Doom is beyond our imagination. Not only will this Earth be destroyed, but the entire Cosmos. So terrible and utter will be the destruction on that Day that even the dead in their tombs will know that the dread Day has come. Yet out of this utter destruction, as these verses remind us, Allah is able to reconstruct all that has lived, ready to face Judgement on the Judgement Day.

(*From* The Essential Teachings of Islam)

Activities

Key Elements

1 What are the five most important things for a Muslim to believe in?
2 Write out the Shahada.
3 Why is idolatry the worst sin in Islam?
4 Why is belief in the One God so important for Muslims?
5 Name one of the angels.
6 Name the five prophets who were rasuls.

7 Why is Muhammad called the 'Seal of the Prophets'?
8 Do Muslims regard Jesus as an important prophet?
9 What does 'Pbuh' stand for and when is it used?
10 In Surah 98, what is referred to as 'Fire of Gehenna'?
11 In the same surah, what is meant by 'Gardens of Eden'?
12 What is Surah 82 about?

Think About It

13 What do you believe about God?

14 What do you believe happens to us after we die?

Further Information

Islam and Christianity

Muhammad seems to have had some good experiences of Christians. Remember Bahira the monk who predicted that he would be a prophet; and Waraqah who encouraged him to believe in his call to prophecy? When persecution drove some of the early Muslims from Makkah, it was to Christian Ethiopia that they went for refuge. The Qur'an states:

You will find the most affectionate among them towards those who believe are those who say: 'We are Christians'.

(*Qur'an 5:82*)

The Qur'an mentions Jesus (called 'Isa) in 15 chapters and in 93 verses. It lists Jesus among the prophets, regarding him as a **rasul**, because he brought the Injil (the Gospel). The baby Jesus is reported to have said:

> *'I am God's servant. He has given me the Book and made me a prophet.'*
>
> *(Qur'an 19:30)*

Like Christianity, Islam believes in the miraculous virgin birth of Jesus to Mary:

> *She said: 'How can I have a boy when no human being has ever touched me, nor am I a loose-living woman?' He said: 'Thus your Lord has said: "It is a simple matter for Me [to do]. We will make him as a sign for mankind and as a mercy from Ourself. It is a matter that has been decided."'*
>
> *(Qur'an 19:20–21)*

But Islam does not believe that Jesus really died on the cross, and therefore does not believe in the resurrection. However, it does believe in his ascension into heaven.

Muslims regard Jesus as sinless but still human, *not divine*. They call him 'son of Mary' *not* 'Son of God'. Because of their firm belief in the oneness of Allah, they are unable to accept any suggestion that God has a son, or that he is three persons, whereas Christians speak of the 'three persons' of the Trinity. (Christians believe that the One God has revealed himself in three roles: as Father, Son and Holy Spirit.)

> *Those who say that God is Christ, the son of Mary, have disbelieved. Christ (himself) said: 'Children of Israel, serve God [who is] my Lord as well as your Lord.' . . . Those who say: 'God is the third of three', have disbelieved. There is no deity except God Alone.*
>
> *(Qur'an 5:72–3)*

There are many points of similarity between these two religions, such as in their ethical teachings and belief in the Day of Judgement; but Muslims regard Islam as a correction and completion of Christianity.

(The above quotations are from *The Qur'an, Basic Teachings*, pp. 118–21.)

Vocabulary

Give the Arabic words for the following:

1 the most popular Muslim greeting
2 someone who has memorised the Qur'an
3 a chapter of the Qur'an
4 'The Opening' – title of the first chapter of the Qur'an
5 collection of reports of what Muhammad said, did or approved
6 the example of the Prophet
7 the declaration of faith – the First Pillar of Islam
8 a statement of faith
9 the oneness of Allah
10 idolatry – associating another being with Allah

Assignments

1 The Qur'an

a) Summarise the main points made about the Qur'an in this chapter.

b) Explain as fully as possible why the Qur'an is so important to Muslims.

c) How far do you think it is necessary to show respect to a holy book belonging to a religion different from your own?

2 Belief in God

a) List all the Names of Allah you can find in Surah 2.

b) Write a paraphrase of Surah 1.

c) What idea of Allah do you have from a) and b)? How does this compare with any other ideas of God which you may have?

3 Life after Death

Look up the following verses from Surah 2, all of which refer to life after death (references are taken from Pickthall's interpretation):

verses 23–5; 62; 81–2; 85b; 126; 160–63; 165; 201; 210; 214; 257.

Make notes of the information they contain, noticing particularly the different titles they use for the Last Day. Use this information (and quotations) to answer the following questions.

a) Describe what the Qur'an teaches about the Last Day and Heaven and Hell.

b) Explain why, according to the Qur'an, some people will be saved and some damned.

c) What effect do you think passages like these have on Muslim readers?

5

Ramadan

Reasons for Fasting

Ramadan is the ninth month of the Islamic calendar. It was during this month that Muhammad received his first revelation of the Qur'an. For this reason, it is a special month for Muslims, which they commemorate by fasting (called **sawm**). Their fasts entail going without food and drink during the daylight hours of every day of the month. Muslims also pay extra attention to the Qur'an during this month; many read it right through from beginning to end.

There are two main reasons why Muslims fast. The first is that it is the Fourth Pillar of Islam (and therefore an obligatory duty and act of worship) commanded for them by Allah in the Qur'an:

O ye who believe! Fasting is prescribed for you, even as it was prescribed for those before you, that you may ward off [evil].

(Pickthall)　　　　　*(Qur'an 2:183)*

The second reason is that Muhammad himself set them the example of fasting:

Ibn 'Umar reported that the people saw the new moon (of Ramadan). So I informed the Messenger of Allah (peace and blessings of Allah be upon him) that I had seen the new moon. Upon this the Holy Prophet observed fasting and ordered the people to observe the fasts of Ramadan.

(Sunan Abu Dawud; Selection of Hadith, No. 55)

Who Must Fast?

Any Muslim who is capable of fasting should do so; but no one should endanger life or health because of it. Consequently, women who are menstruating, pregnant, or breast-feeding should not fast. Nor should people who are ill and could make themselves worse by fasting.

Muslim soldiers, or people on long journeys, will need to keep up their strength and so they are also excused from fasting.

These people should try to make up the fast-days they have missed, at another time. If they cannot do this, then they should give the cost of two meals to the poor, for each fast-day they miss, if they can afford to do so.

Elderly people are not expected to fast, but they too are asked to feed the poor instead, if they can afford it.

Young children will gradually be introduced to fasting, perhaps for just half a day at first. Once they reach the age of puberty, they will have to do the same fasts as the adults. This is often taken to apply from 12 years old.

Lastly, the insane are not required to fast. They would not understand what was going on, and would not be able to gain any spiritual benefit from this religious duty, but would simply be given unnecessary suffering.

When is the Fast?

Fasting goes on every day of the month of Ramadan (29/30 days). The Muslim calendar is based on the moon, and the sighting of the new moon marks the beginning of each new month. The lunar year is 11 days shorter than the Western year (which is based on the sun), so the Muslim months rotate backwards, each year, through the seasons. Fasting takes place during daylight hours, from dawn (about two hours before sunrise) until sunset. When Ramadan falls in summer, the days can be very long in some countries, and the fasting is particularly demanding. (Muslims in the 'Lands of the midnight sun' have a problem because, in mid-summer, there is no night-time! They usually fast from 6 a.m. to 6 p.m.)

Muslim months begin with the sighting of the new moon. Here there is rejoicing at the end of the month of Ramadan.

Doing Without

A typical fast-day begins very early in the morning, because Muslims get up to have something to drink and something nourishing to eat before the fast begins. In the winter, when nights are long, this early morning meal is often quite substantial. But in the summer, it might have to be eaten only a few hours after finishing the night meal, and will therefore be quite light. High-energy foods are usually eaten, such as yoghurt, cheese and honey. Spicy foods are avoided, because they make people extra thirsty.

In many Muslim countries, people are woken up in time for this meal by drum-beaters or by cannon-fire. In non-Muslim countries, they follow the timetables issued by the mosques, and have to rely on their own alarm clocks to wake them.

During the day, it will be difficult for Muslims who are fasting to continue with their normal work, particularly anything strenuous; the whole pace of life slows down in Muslim countries. It is more difficult, of course, in non-Muslim countries, if no allowance is made. The following advice is given to teachers in Britain:

> *Children who are fasting may feel weak and tired during the day, especially in the afternoon. Strenuous physical exercise may make them feel worse.... Those children who go swimming may be concerned about swallowing water – strictly speaking this would be breaking the fast – so they will spit it out.*
>
> *Teachers should avoid giving the impression that fasting is 'a nuisance, disruptive to school routine and work', but should view it as something positive. They must accept that a child's attitudes, behaviour and performance may in some cases be affected, but that these changes are purely temporary. They should acknowledge their acceptance of fasting by showing interest and asking questions about fasting routines. They should accept that Britain is a multi-religious and multi-cultural society; tolerance and respect should be given to the other's faith and culture.*

(The Muslim Guide, p. 49)

Nadia, a young Muslim girl, describes her difficulties in keeping the fast (of over 18 hours) while at school in Britain. We take up the story at morning break.

As Fouzia had told most of my friends that I was fasting, I didn't expect anybody to offer me any crisps but I received exactly the opposite. Nearly all my friends offered me something, but I refused. . . .

'Is it easy to fast?' asked Shanie.

'The answer is No, but I try my best to keep faith in God and I shall hopefully complete today's fast.' [. . .]

Jane and I started walking around the playground. She had some sweets and was kind enough not to offer me any.

Walking about, Jane asked me, 'Don't you get thirsty or hungry?'

'Of course I do, but I'm not very hungry yet, my mouth is dry though.'

'Shall we go to the cloakroom?' Jane suggested.

'Good idea!' I exclaimed. We went to the cloakroom. Jane had a drink but I could only rinse my mouth.

A couple of minutes later we went back to class. We had maths till quarter past twelve. Then it was lunchtime.

I could see people lining up for school lunch.

Hayley asked me, 'Are you having packed lunch or school lunch?'

'Neither,' I replied, 'because I am fasting and I can't eat or drink anything till twenty past nine in the evening, precisely nine hours from now.'

We played together for a while until the whistle went for packed lunch people, so I played with Fouzia and other friends who had finished their lunch. As we were playing a first year girl came up to me and started teasing me. . . .

'Would you like some cream cakes or jam doughnuts, maybe some chocolates, you might like some currant buns,' she began. 'I think sweets and crisps are nice, too,' she finished. I was really getting angry. I don't know how people could be so ignorant.

(*Eid Mubarak*, pp. 12–14)

Nadia Bakhsh was only ten years old when she wrote her book *Eid Mubarak*, from which this passage is taken. Despite the difficulties described here, she says that she enjoyed her first fast so much that she wanted everyone to know what it felt like for a child to fast.

Fasting can be even more difficult for Western converts to Islam who have not been brought up to do it. The following passage describes how one particular man came through it.

Past my mid-forties and an Englishman accustomed to eating more than necessary and smoking like a chimney, I approached Ramadan with a fast growing apprehension. . . . I had ideas of going to Morocco to escape the temptations of England but it was not the Will of Allah. In answer to my prayers for help, I remained in England and taught a group of Muslim students. From them I learned to fast. From Allah I was given strength to fulfil both my spiritual and teaching obligations without great distress. On the contrary, at the permitted times for eating, after sunset and at dawn, Muslims make this a time for close and kindly relationships. My next Ramadan? I am apprehensive but I now know the energy and help to expect from worship – it is the Reward of Ramadan.

(*The Muslim Guide*, p. 27)

Not only must Muslims give up food and drink, but also sexual relations and smoking (during daylight hours). If you have ever known someone trying to give up smoking, you will appreciate how difficult this can be.

Muslims are also supposed to give up bad thoughts and wrongdoings during Ramadan. Not that these things are excusable at any time, but this special month reminds Muslims to be particularly careful about living up to the high moral standards of their religion. Also, because all Muslims are fasting together, there is a greater sense of comradeship than at some other times, and therefore unpleasantness to one another is less likely.

Typical Programme of Lectures and Discussions Held at the London Central Mosque During Ramadan

Ramadan	Subject	Speaker
1	Ahkam of Fasting	Sh. Zahran Ibrahim
2	Ahkam of Fasting	Sh. Hamid Khalifa
3	Ahkam of Fasting	Sh. Gamal Manna'a
4	The Rules of Recitation and its Obligations 'Tajweed'	Sh. Mahmoud Hammad
5	Revelation of the Qur'an	Br. Salah Ghobashy
6	Collection & Recording of the Qur'an	Br. Ismail Abdul Halim
7	The Veracity of the Qur'an	Sh. Zahran Ibrahim
8	The Qur'an and the People of the Book	Mr Hisham El Essawy
9	The Sword and Islam	Sh. Salah Jannah
10	The Battle of the Ditch and the Conspiracy of the Jews	Br. Mohammad Ali Shayal
11	Fath Makkah	Br. Osama Badra
12	Qur'an as the Prime Source of Law	Sh. Gamal Manna'a
13	The Eternal and Universal Relevance of the Qur'an	Dr Mohammad Abdul Haleem
14	Al-Sunnah – Definition and Recording	Imam Mahmoud Mirpuri
15	Al-Sunnah – Methodology of Collection	Sh. Shuayb Hassan
16	Ethics, Morality and Behaviour as Derived from the Sunnah	Khwaja Qamaruddin
17	Consequences of Badr	Sh. Abdullah Azzouabi
18	Glimpse of the Prophets Practices in Ramadan	Sh. Mohamed Osman
19	al-Itikaaf	Imam Abu Said
20	Al-Sunnah – Its Place and Necessity in Islam	Dr Fathi Osman
21	Zakaat – Remedy for Poverty	Dr Mohammad Khalid
22	Zakaat-ul-Fitr and its Significance	Sh. Hamid Khalifa
23	Spiritual Upliftment in Islam	Br. Hassan Gai Eaton
24	The Acceptance of Supplication in Ramadan	Br. Yusuf Islam
25	Spiritual Solace of the Qur'an	Br. Saad Al-Barazi
26	Laylatul Qadr	Dr Manazir Ahsan
27	Farewell to Ramadan	Br. Abdul Jalil Sajid
28	Arabic – Lingua Franca of Islam	Br. Salah Ghobashy
29	Special Educational Needs of Muslim Children	Dr G. N. Saqib

Activities

Key Elements

1 Give two reasons why Muslims should fast.

2 Here is a list of people who are excused from the Ramadan fast: the old, the young, soldiers, travellers, women during their periods, nursing mothers. Which three are missing?

3 What is a lunar calendar based on (as opposed to a solar calendar)?

4 If Ramadan began on 11 January 1997, when would it be expected to start in 1998?

5 How long does each day's fast last?

Doing Extra

This special month is also a chance to give more attention to prayer and the reading of the Qur'an. Many Muslims perform an extra prayer with either eight or twenty rak'ahs, after the night prayer. Mosques arrange extra opportunities for people to learn about their religion, as is shown by the programme of daily lectures throughout Ramadan, at the London Central Mosque.

Many Muslims make a special effort to attend congregational prayers at the mosque each day – not just on Fridays. Food is provided to break the fast for those who attend the sunset prayer. Some Muslims stay at the mosque for the last ten days of the month, during which **Laylat-ul-Qadr** is celebrated. The Night of Power is normally accepted to have been on the 27th of the month, but tradition says that it was at least during these last ten days. Those on this religious retreat spend the time in religious study, prayer and meditation.

Meal Times

Although no food may be eaten during the day, food is still bought and sold, and women have to prepare food for the night-time. Like the preparations for any celebration, this can be an exhausting time for them, which continues throughout the month.

As each day's fast draws to its close, Muslims feel excited, proud of their endurance, and very hungry and thirsty. They wait for the announcement on television or radio, or by means of a call from the minaret, that sunset has come. Then they break their fast with **iftar** (breakfast). They eat very little at first, to get their digestive systems gradually used to food again. They will drink a glass of water,

A Turkish family shares a meal together at the end of a day in Ramadan.

or a sweet drink to quench their thirst and restore some of their energy. It is traditional to eat sweet dates, or the popular 'stars of the moon', which are dried apricots that have soaked all day in sugar water.

The **Maghrib** prayer is said before the main meal is eaten. Sometimes this meal is left until late at night, and may take the form of an elaborate dinner party. Those who have kept the fast together throughout the day now celebrate together at night. The poor are given food or invited to share a meal, so that they too can enjoy the pleasures of Ramadan. At the London Central Mosque, for example, people donate money to provide a banquet every night during Ramadan for 2000 lonely, single or needy Muslims.

Children too, in Muslim countries, enter into the party spirit. They go round the streets with candle-lit lanterns, singing songs at people's doors and being rewarded with money and sweets.

Non-Muslims sometimes think it is strange that Muslims should go without food all day, and then make up for it at night. But it is the discipline of it which is important, rather than the fact of going without. Islam does not teach people to go to extremes; it knows our body's needs, and does not ask more than is humanly possible or advisable. As with the case of those who are excused fasting, the Qur'an says: 'He (Allah) desireth not hardship for you' (2:185).

People enjoy the food all the more because they have gone without it earlier; they join in the celebrations, because they feel they have deserved them. But what about those Muslims who did not manage to keep the fast? Some may have broken it by accident, such as swallowing a mouthful of water while in the shower, or eating a sweet from a friend without thinking. They can make up for this if they wish with an extra day's fast after the Festival. It is much more serious when Muslims give way to temptation and break the fast on purpose. To make up for this, they should fast for 60 consecutive days. If their health will not permit this, then they can pay for a meal for 60 poor people.

In any religious community, there are always some who are non-practising. But, in Muslim countries, there is a lot of social pressure on everyone to fast, even if they do not keep other religious rules. Even in Britain, where Muslims are a minority in a secular society, between 75 and 80 per cent of them keep Ramadan.

Supermarkets are busy in Muslim countries during Ramadan as people prepare for the evening meal.

Benefits of Fasting

If you are asked the purpose of **sawm**, this can include both the reasons for fasting and its benefits. Reasons why Muslims fast are given at the beginning of this chapter. Here are some of the benefits that Muslims may gain from fasting.

1 There is a feeling of togetherness, as all Muslims, rich and poor, fulfil the same demands of the fast and then share their food together at night.

An Arab businessman, who had arrived at the mosque in a chauffeur-driven blue Rolls-Royce and was sitting in obvious discomfort while listening to the lesson from the Imam before the sunset prayer, said: 'When you see the wealthy, the powerful and the famous sitting on the carpeted floor next to the poor and eating the same food, you see the true spirit of equality which Islam has brought to mankind.'

(The Independent, 2 May 1988)

2 The rich gain a better understanding of what it must be like for the poor who cannot always eat when they want to. This should make them more generous towards them.

In fasting they have the chance to share some of the anguish of hunger and poverty experienced by the distressed and destitute of the world. From this experience, they learn to be increasingly grateful and generous.

(The Muslim Guide, p. 26)

3 Muslims will learn to appreciate all the good things they have each day, and to thank Allah for them, instead of just taking them for granted.

4 They will learn self-control.

Over-indulgence in eating, drinking and marital relations makes one the slave of desires and habits. It is believed that fasting frees one from this slavery. The purpose of fasting in Islam is to control passions and thus making one a person of good deeds and intentions.

(From Islam. Sawm and Hajj*)*

5 They will learn how to endure hardships.

Just as we might go to the dentist and put up with a certain amount of suffering because we know it is necessary for our health and well-being, so the Muslim regards Ramadan. Putting up with a small amount of hardship teaches a person to have patience and perseverance and develops the qualities of courage and steadfastness in the face of difficulties.

(Ramadan and Id-ul-Fitr, p. 13)

6 Throughout the month, they will be reminded constantly of the importance of worshipping Allah, not just for this life, but for eternity.

Salman Al-Farisi reported that the Messenger of Allah (peace and blessings of Allah be upon him) addressed us on the last day of Sha'ban and said: 'O people, a great and blessed month is near at hand. . . . It is the month of endurance and the reward of endurance is Paradise.'

(Shu'ab Al-Iman; Selection from Hadith, No. 61, pp. 34–5)

Activities

Key Elements

1 Why do Muslims usually get up early before the fast begins?
2 Why was it especially difficult for Nadia to fast?
3 Why was it especially difficult for the Englishman to fast?
4 Why is it likely to be more difficult for Muslim women to fast than for men?
5 Name four things Muslims have to abstain from during the fast.
6 Name two extra things that Muslims should do during Ramadan?
7 Why should we expect Muslims to get on better during Ramadan?
8 How do Muslims break their fast at the end of the day?
9 Why is there a party-spirit at night time during Ramadan?

10   There are six benefits from fasting listed on p. 53. Which do you think is most important?
11   How could you help a Muslim classmate who was fasting?
12   What things do we often take for granted? Does going without help

us to appreciate things more?
13   How far do you think fasting helps people to understand the poor and starving?
14   What is the value of testing our self-control?

Id-ul-Fitr

'Is it Id? Is it Id tomorrow?' I asked anxiously.

'We don't know yet,' my mum said. My dad then had a good idea.

'I'll phone the Islamic Cultural Centre (Regents Park Mosque, London). They often have the latest information.' My dad phoned but it was engaged. . . .

It took some time to get to sleep but I eventually did. It was difficult to sleep because of the excitement of Id, whether it was on or not.

I woke up early and went downstairs to see if there were any Id cards. There were a few so I took them upstairs to my parents who opened them. One of the envelopes contained £5. It was from Pakistan. The money was for me as an Idi from my grandmum. I displayed all the cards on the mantelpiece.

I asked my mum and dad, 'Is it Id? Is it Id today? Please tell me!'

My mum spoke next, 'We phoned at 3 o'clock this morning, and found out it's Id!'

'Hooray! Hooray!' I was so pleased. 'Id Mubarak,' I said to both my mum and dad.

(Eid Mubarak, pp. 24 and 27)

Islamic greetings cards. They wish people 'Id Mubarak' which means a 'Blessed' or 'Happy Festival'.

Imagine going to bed on what you thought was Christmas Eve, not knowing for sure if it really would be Christmas the next day! Yet that is the uncertainty Muslims have to live with at Id-ul-Fitr. Each Islamic month begins at new moon. Islamic calendars are based on the probable visibility of the new moon by the naked eye; but festivals cannot be observed until the new moon is *actually* seen by at least two witnesses. Calendars therefore include the proviso 'Subject to the sighting of the moon'.

In Muslim countries, people usually stay

up at the end of Ramadan, and when they see the new moon of the month of Shawwal, there is great rejoicing. Cannon fire used to boom out the message that the month of fasting had finished and the festival had begun. Now it is more usual for it to be announced on the radio and television. In the West, a cloudy sky frequently obscures the moon. So Muslims here have to rely on the message coming through to their centres from Muslim countries like Morocco (which is nearest to Britain).

Id-ul-Fitr means 'Festival of Fast Breaking'. It is the most popular festival of all, especially with the children who get lots of presents, money, sweets and new clothes. The intensity of the whole month of fasting has been leading up to this. The preparations involve all the trappings we associate with celebrations (or most of them): decorating the house, sending cards, buying and wrappings gifts, wearing our best clothes, and preparing special food. (Westerners might notice the absence of alcohol.)

Remembering that this is a religious festival, families attend mosque in the morning for special Id prayers. So many people go that extra space has to be found, often outside, where sheets or mats are laid down on the ground. At some big centres it is also necessary for a number of services to be held in relay, as shown by these five morning services held at the London Central Mosque.

Time for Id Prayers

1st Prayer	6.00 a.m.
2nd Prayer	7.30 a.m.
3rd Prayer	9.00 a.m.
4th Prayer	10.00 a.m.
5th Prayer	11.00 a.m.

Important instructions for Id day, issued by the London Central Mosque.

In order to derive the maximum benefit from the great day of thanksgiving and rejoicing that is Id-ul-Fitr and in order that the Salat should be conducted in as serene and orderly manner as possible, we kindly request worshippers to observe the following instructions.

Please perform Wudu before coming to the Mosque.

- All worshippers are requested to observe proper Islamic dress on this occasion in particular and at all times. Ladies are reminded that Islamic dress requires them to cover their body with the exception of the face and hands. Transparent clothing is not allowed.

- On reaching the mosque, observe Police parking instructions. Come in time and park away from the mosque to avoid congestion. No parking is allowed on the mosque premises. Cars parked in Park Road or Hanover Gate are at risk of being removed by the Police.

- Please follow the signs at the mosque in order to avoid congestion.

- A one-way system has been devised where worshippers are required to enter the Prayer Halls by the main gates and leave by the other exits indicated.

- Ladies are particularly requested to observe the one-way system as facilities are inadequate for large numbers at the mosque.

- Please use the polythene bags provided to keep your shoes with you and discard the bags together with other litter in the bins provided. Keep the mosque premises clean.

- Attendants are available for any assistance. Please help them to help you.

- Children lost in the crowd must be reported to the Lost and Found Centre Point located underneath the flats.

- Please remember that the Khutbah in Arabic and English is part of Salat al-Id and worshippers should sit quietly until the Khutbah is complete. Please do not talk during the Khutbah as this invalidates the Prayers.

- When you have finished the Id prayer, please leave the premises as quickly as possible for the next session of worshippers.

May Allah accept your Prayer and grant you all the blessings of Id.

Zakah

Righteous is he who believeth in Allah ... and giveth his wealth, for love of Him, to kinsfolk and to orphans and the needy and the wayfarer and to those who ask, and to set slaves free; and observeth proper worship and payeth the poor-due.

(Pickthall)   (Qur'an 2:177)

Lo! those who believe and do good works and establish worship and pay the poor-due, their reward is with their Lord and there shall no fear come upon them neither shall they grieve.

(Pickthall)   (Qur'an 2:277)

When the prayers are over, the parties begin. Friends and families get together, call on one another and forget old quarrels. This should be a time of *peace* (the meaning of 'Islam'). Birthdays that fall during Ramadan are celebrated at Id-ul-Fitr; and a good number of weddings take place on Id days. During all these family celebrations, many Muslims also remember relatives who have died, and visit their graves.

Muhammad called Id-ul-Fitr the 'Day of Reward', coming as it does after the trials of Ramadan. Muslims thank Allah for giving them the strength to endure the fast. Now they can relax and enjoy all the good things that Allah has given them. In Muslim countries, this is a national holiday of between two and four days long. In Western countries, Muslims take a day off work or school.

Yet another name for Id-ul-Fitr is the 'Festival of Charity' because steps are taken to make sure that the poor, too, can enjoy good food at this time. Every Muslim who can afford it pays **Zakat-ul-Fitr**. This special religious tax for the Id is the cost of a meal per head. This charity should be paid before the Id prayer, showing that there are times when caring for others takes priority even over prayer. Usually, it is paid several days beforehand so that it can be distributed in good time for the festival.

Many Muslims pay **Zakah** at this time (as well as Zakat-ul-Fitr). Zakah is an obligatory poor-tax, or poor-due. It is so important that it is set beside worship in the quotations above. Indeed, it is regarded as an act of worship itself, since it is the Third Pillar of Islam.

Zakah is a type of charity to help the needy in Islam; but Muslims prefer to use the words 'poor-due', since people have a duty to pay it and the poor have a right to receive it (and should not refuse it when it is offered). It is given to those in need, such as poor families, students, and even Islamic organisations in need of financial assistance. It is a relatively small tax of about 2.5% of a person's wealth. (There are complicated rules for working it out.) Those who have no surplus wealth are not required to pay Zakah, but will be the recipients of it.

In some Islamic countries, Zakah is collected by the government; in others it is regarded as a private matter. Muslims in the West often send money to those in Third World countries, like Bangladesh, showing the sense of brotherhood between Muslims throughout the world.

Zakah is Islam's way of redistributing wealth, to make a fairer society. Islam teaches that all our blessings come from Allah, and we should show our gratitude both by enjoying them ourselves, and also by sharing them with others. The word *zakah* means 'purification'. Muslims believe that giving some of their wealth helps to purify them of greed and selfishness. Zakah also aims to purify society of the evil divisions between rich and poor.

Many Muslims will want to give away more than the required amount, and their religion encourages them to do so. Voluntary charity is called **sadaqah**.

> *Spend your wealth for the cause of Allah, and be not cast by your own hands to ruin; and do good. Lo! Allah loveth the beneficent.*
>
> *(Pickthall)*   *(Qur'an 2:195)*

Zakah is about giving away money (unless you are on the receiving end); but what does Islam teach about gaining money?

- It can be inherited, but there are rules to make sure that this is distributed fairly.
- Most money should be earned by honest work.
- Money should not simply make more money, for example, through investment (otherwise the rich will just get richer all the time).

Activities

Key Elements

1 Give three English titles for Id-ul-Fitr.
2 Explain why it is sometimes called the Day of Reward.
3 When does Id-ul-Fitr start?
4 Why do Muslims attend mosque at Id-ul-Fitr?
5 What is Zakat-ul-Fitr used for?
6 What is Zakah?
7 Explain the meaning of the word 'zakah'.
8 What percentage of a Muslim's money is given annually for Zakah?

Think About It

9 Do you think we should give money to charity? Try to give arguments both for and against before coming to your own conclusion.

Further Information

Sevian

It is traditional for Pakistani Muslims to eat **sevian** for breakfast on Id-ul-Fitr. This is vermicelli, long thin threads of pasta which can be boiled, fried or cooked in milk. This is the milk-pudding recipe.

Ingredients
50 g (2 oz) Butter
3 Crushed cardamom seeds
75 g (3 oz) Vermicelli
100 g (4 oz) Sugar
250 ml (¹/₂ pint) Milk
Pinch of Saffron powder

To decorate
6 almonds (blanched)
6 pistachios (unblanched)

Method

Heat butter and crushed cardamom seeds in a saucepan until the fat has melted. Fry vermicelli for about five minutes. Do not burn. (Pakistani vermicelli is much darker in colour than the European. If pale coloured vermicelli is used, the frying should turn it golden brown.) When the mixture has cooled, add the sugar and milk and bring to the boil. Lower the heat and put the lid on the pan, stirring occasionally to prevent sticking. Uncover the pan and cook the mixture until dry. This is a matter of taste: some prefer a more creamy texture, leaving some liquid. Add the saffron and stir very well. Serve on a plate and garnish with shredded almonds and pistachios.

(The Id-ul-Fitr Book, pp. 36–7)

Vocabulary

Give the Arabic words for the following:
1 name of the holy month
2 fasting
3 breakfast
4 name of the festival which marks the end of Ramadan
5 festival
6 happy/blessed
7 the poor-due
8 voluntary charity

Assignments

1 Fasting

a) Write out a full day's timetable for a Muslim teenager during Ramadan. Beside it, write out a timetable for the same day for his or her non-Muslim friend.

b) Give as many reasons as possible why this Muslim teenager is fasting.

c) What do you think is the greatest benefit he or she will gain from Ramadan?

2 Id-ul-Fitr

a) Select five things Muslims do to celebrate Id-ul-Fitr. Write a short account of the festival, describing these five things. You can also illustrate them if you want to. (N.B. Select a variety of things, so that you are able to answer the next part of the question fully.)

b) Id-ul-Fitr is a religious festival. Explain the religious significance of each of the five things you have described in a).

c) Why is it that people often want to celebrate together, when they have been through a difficult time together? Can you give any other (non-religious) examples of this?

3 Wealth

a) Read Surah 2:261–281 and look for these ideas:

- Allah sees what you give.
- You should not give to charity just to show off.
- If you do good with your money, Allah will reward you.
- Give to help the poor who cannot work.
- Allah allows you to make money by working, for example, trading; but you should not make money just by charging interest on a loan (usury).
- If someone owes you money and cannot pay it back, give him time or, better still, let him keep it.

Are there any other ideas about wealth in these verses?

b) 'What I do with my money is my affair.' Try to give an Islamic response to this statement.

c) Say whether you agree or disagree with each of the statements in both a) and b) above, giving your reasons.

6

Pilgrimage

Reasons for Pilgrimage

A pilgrim is someone who travels to a holy place, for religious devotions. The most important place of pilgrimage for Muslims is, of course, Makkah. Not only was Muhammad born in Makkah and lived there most of his life, but he himself performed religious rituals there. Makkah had been a holy city long before Muhammad reclaimed it for Allah. He encouraged the continuation of many of the old practices, but purified them by restoring what he believed to be their true meaning, in the worship of the One God. So pilgrims to Makkah are walking in the footsteps of Muhammad, performing the same rituals that he did on pilgrimage all those years ago.

Even more important than following the Prophet's example, is the fact that pilgrimage is commanded in the Qur'an.

Perform the pilgrimage and the visit (to Mecca) for Allah.
(Pickthall)   *(Qur'an 2:196)*

It is the duty of all men towards God to come to the House a pilgrim, if he is able to make his way there.
(Arberry)   *(Qur'an 3:93)*

And proclaim among men the Pilgrimage, and they shall come unto thee on foot and upon every lean beast, they shall come from every deep ravine.
(Arberry)   *(Qur'an 22:27)*

The Fifth Pillar of Islam makes it an obligation (**fard**) for all Muslims to perform the Greater Pilgrimage at least once in their lives, if possible. To fail to do so, when they are able, is regarded as a grave sin. Yet only about one in ten Muslims manages to do it, because they have to fulfil the following requirements.

- They must have reached the age of responsibility and be of sound mind, so that they know what they are doing. Although children are sometimes taken with their parents on pilgrimage, this does not count for them as fulfilling the Fifth Pillar.
- They must be able to afford it. Therefore, they should have no debts; and they should have gained the money to pay for the pilgrimage through honest means.
- They should be physically fit. It is advisable for Muslims to go on pilgrimage when they are young enough to withstand the gruelling conditions. Unfortunately, many cannot afford it until their old age, and some die on the pilgrimage.

The Greater Pilgrimage is called the **Hajj**; those who manage to complete it are honoured with the titles of **hajji** (for a man) and **hajja** (for a woman). The word **hajj** literally means 'to set out for a definite purpose'. As you read the rest of this chapter, think about its meaning and importance for Muslims – its religious purpose.

Hajj: the Greater Pilgrimage

The Greater Pilgrimage is called the **Hajj**, and this can only be done on special days during the pilgrimage month, Dhul-Hijjah. This is what it involves.

- Wearing the ihram.
- Travelling towards 'Arafat on 8 Dhul-Hijjah (and staying at Mina overnight).
- 'Standing' at 'Arafat from noon to dusk on 9 Dhul Hijja.
- 'Stoning the Devil' and making an animal sacrifice at Mina on 10 Dhul Hijja.
- Cutting or shaving the hair.
- Making the Tawaf, the 'Circling' of the Ka'bah in Makkah.
- Further 'Stoning of the Devil' at Mina on 11, 12 (and 13) Dhul Hijja.

When a pilgrim finally leaves Makkah (after 'Umrah or Hajj), he or she will perform a Farewell Circling of the Ka'bah.

The Hajj itself takes only 5–6 days, but pilgrims will need time to perform the 'Umrah as well (notice that this means doing some rituals twice), and will therefore arrive in Makkah some days before 8 Dhul-Hijjah. Many, coming from afar on this journey of a lifetime, like to extend the trip to have more time at Makkah and Mina, and to go on to visit Madinah, the second holy city in Islam. In 1998, a Hajj travel agent in London charged pilgrims £1850 for a complete two-week package, or £2200 for a three-week package. Other package deals could be found in cheaper hotels from £1100.

A hajji's house.

'Umrah: the Lesser Pilgrimage

On visiting Makkah, at any time of the year, Muslims are required to perform the **'Umrah**, the Lesser Pilgrimage. This is what it involves.

- Wearing the **ihram**, the pilgrim's clothes, before approaching Makkah.
- Making the **Tawaf**, the ritual 'Circling' of the Ka'bah seven times.
- Making the **Sa'y**, the ritual 'Running' between Mounts As-Safa and Al-Marwa seven times.

At Makkah

The Qur'an calls Makkah 'the mother town' (42:7) because it is the spiritual centre of Islam. Each year at Hajj, pilgrims arrive there in their hundreds of thousands, by road, sea and air. As they approach Makkah, there are signs warning that only Muslims are allowed into the holy city. The area of the Hajj is **haram**. This word means both 'forbidden' and 'sacred', i.e. it is so special that it is set apart for a holy purpose, and those who are not Muslims are therefore forbidden. The mosque in which the Ka'bah stands is called the **Masjid al-Haram**, the Sacred Mosque. The boundary lies between about 5 and 30 kilometres from the Ka'bah; and everyone is stopped on the approaches to the city, to have their passes checked.

Ihram

Before reaching the sacred city, pilgrims must purify their bodies (preferably with a full bath, or else by performing wudu, see p. 14f), and enter into a state of holiness called **ihram**. This word literally means 'consecration', or dedication to holy things. The special dress worn by pilgrims is also called ihram. For men, it consists of two pieces of unsewn white cloth: one tied round the waist, the other thrown over the left shoulder. They

Pilgrims in ihram dress reach Makkah.

have nothing on their heads (which is why many carry umbrellas, for protection against the sun), and are only permitted to have sandals on their feet. There is no such uniform for women, but they must be fully covered, apart from the hands and face. Many wear simple long white dresses with head-scarves.

Ihram is an important symbol for Muslims. It has the following meanings.

- They have entered a state of holiness. It is a reminder that they are performing special, sacred rituals.
- They have put off all that connects them with their usual lives, in order to concentrate totally on Allah.
- Dressed so simply, it is a sign of humility before Allah.
  (The ihram clothes are similar to those in which a new-born child is wrapped. They can therefore remind a Muslim of the day he first came into the world as a helpless baby. Also, the ihram wraps will be kept for the pilgrim's burial. So wearing them now reminds the pilgrim

that he comes before Allah, stripped of all material goods and status, just as he will be at death.)

- White is a symbol of purity. It is a reminder that they must try not to sin.
- Muslims are all dressed the same because they are equal in the sight of Allah.

Once in the state of ihram, pilgrims must not worry over their personal appearance, so they cannot wear perfume or jewellery. They must be particularly mindful of Allah's laws, and must therefore avoid all violence, even to animals, plants and insects. They must treat the pilgrimage as a sacrifice to Allah, and must abstain from sexual relationships during that time. (Many husbands and wives travel together, but stay in separate accommodation.) In short, they must devote themselves wholly to Allah for this brief but intense period of their lives. This is expressed in the frequent pilgrim calls in Arabic which mean 'Doubly at your service, O God'.

Makkah is now part of modern Saudi Arabia, and the king is the guardian of the Muslim shrines there. Each year the Saudi government goes to great trouble to organise and accommodate all the pilgrims. In Makkah, they are divided into groups with an official guide to look after them and instruct them in the rituals.

Further Information

Security Problems with the Hajj

These news-cuttings indicate some of the problems facing the Saudi Arabian government in its guardianship of the pilgrim sites.

300 feared dead as fire sweeps Mecca tent city

Disaster struck the annual pilgrimage to Mecca yesterday, when as many as 300 people died in a terrifying fire.

. . .

In 1994, hundreds of Indonesian pilgrims were killed when they surged forward in the ceremony of 'stoning the devil' which is part of the Hajj ritual. In 1990, 1,426 people were crushed to death in a tunnel leading to holy sites and in 1987, 402 Iranians were killed in a fight with Saudi security forces.

Over the past ten years Saudi Arabia has spent $18.6bn (£11.4bn) providing facilities for the pilgrims. Some 150,000 security forces, guides and boy scouts have been mobilised by the kingdom to oversee the Hajj, the largest gathering of people in the world.

About half of the 2 million pilgrims are foreign – some 60,000 of them Iranian – and the rest Saudi Arabian. Saudi Arabian Airlines has transported an estimated 600,000 pilgrims from 60 destinations around the world.

(*The Independent*, 16 April 1997)

Activities

Key Elements

1 What is pilgrimage?
2 Why should Muslims go on Hajj?
3 List the conditions a Muslim must fulfil before he or she can perform an acceptable Hajj.
4 When does Hajj have to be performed?
5 In which country is Makkah?
6 Why is Makkah the most important city in Islam?

7 Why is Madinah the second holy city in Islam?
8 Describe the male pilgrim's dress.
9 Which parts of their bodies should women pilgrims leave uncovered?
10 What does the wearing of ihram signify? (Five meanings are given in the text.)

Think About It

11 What makes 'a journey of a lifetime'?
12 Why do you think pilgrimage is described as both an outward and an inner journey?

13 How important do you think uniforms are (such as ihram)?
14 Do you think Muslims are right to ban non-Muslims from their holiest sites?

Saudis clear debris of Mecca's hellish pilgrimage inferno

The Saudi Arabian authorities in Mecca were yesterday trying to identify the bodies of 343 Muslim pilgrims who burned to death in the fire which engulfed their tent city as they attended the Hajj pilgrimage.

A further 1,290 people are known to have suffered injuries as the flames, fanned by the wind, spread rapidly through the 70,000 tents pitched on the plain of Mina outside the holy city of Mecca.

. . .

In the remains of the Mina encampment, trucks were beginning yesterday to cart away burned wreckage of everything from charred water bottles to refrigerators, air conditioners and buses, which caught fire as strong winds spread the flames. The cause of the blaze is being attributed to an exploding gas cylinder, often used for cooking food and making coffee and tea by many of the two million Hajj pilgrims.

(*The Independent*, 17 April 1997)

Mecca: the aftermath

The Koran is unequivocal. It permits no violence during the holy pilgrimage to Mecca. Indeed, even *en route*, Muslims must take care to avoid crushing insects underfoot. So the riot that took place on the night of July 31, in which 402 people died, was particularly devastating both to devout followers of Allah and their political leaders. . . .

The Sunday Times has pieced together the events that left 275 Iranians, 85 Saudis and 42 others dead and 649 injured. Our investigation suggests that the violent demonstration by Iranian pilgrims was preplanned, but that the Saudi police over-reacted in their efforts to maintain order.

(*The Sunday Times*, 9 August 1987)

An aerial view over tent city.

The Ka'bah

The first thing that any Muslim pilgrim will want to see is the building towards which he or she turns in prayer five times a day: the holy Ka'bah. Set in the courtyard of the

Sacred Mosque in Makkah, it is 15.25 metres high, made of large stone blocks, and cube-shaped (ka'bah means 'cube'). It is covered with a beautiful black silk cloth, called the **Kiswah**. This is made in Makkah and has words of the Qur'an embroidered on it in gold thread. The edges of the Kiswah are hoisted up during the Hajj; and towards the end of Hajj, on 10 Dhul-Hijjah, it is replaced each year with a new one. The old cloth is cut up and sent to various Muslim organisations throughout the world. It is regarded as a great honour to be able to frame a piece and hang it on the wall.

For a Muslim, the Ka'bah has layer upon layer of tradition and meaning attached to it. It is said to be the first house of prayer on earth. Legend has it that Adam was sent down from heaven and wandered the earth until he reached Arabia. There he wanted to build a house of prayer like the one in heaven. One story says that Allah let down a replica out of heaven; others that Adam built it himself.

Later, Ibrahim is said to have rebuilt the Ka'bah, with the help of his son Isma'il. The Station of Ibrahim now stands in the court-yard of the Sacred Mosque, marking the spot from which it is believed he began the building operations. Tradition tells that Ibrahim also prayed at this spot, and pilgrims are required to do the same.

And when We made the House (at Mecca) a resort for mankind and a sanctuary, (saying): Take as your place of worship the place where Abraham stood (to pray). And We imposed a duty upon Abraham and Ishmael, (saying): Purify My house for those who go around and those who meditate therein and those who bow down and prostrate themselves (in worship).

(Pickthall)   (Qur'an 2:125)

The Station of Ibrahim. It contains a boulder on which he is said to have stood when directing the building operations for the Ka'bah.

Ibrahim's Egyptian wife was called Hajar, who bore him Isma'il, his eldest son. There is an open area in front of the Ka'bah, enclosed by a semi-circular wall, marking the traditional site of the graves of Hajar and Isma'il.

Low down, set into the wall in one corner of the Ka'bah, is the Black Stone. It is a very ancient stone, probably a meteorite (it is believed to have come down from heaven). One tradition is that it was originally white, but turned black as a result of people's sin.

There is a story about the Black Stone and Muhammad when he was a young man in Makkah. The Ka'bah was being repaired and the Black Stone had been removed. When the time came to replace it, the four leading families in Makkah argued over who should have the privilege. They finally agreed that it should be decided by the next person to enter the Sacred Mosque – and that was Muhammad. With great diplomacy, Muhammad refused to choose a representative from any one family. Instead, he told each to take hold of a corner of a cloak in which the stone would be carried to the Ka'bah. Then Muhammad himself lifted out the stone and restored it to its place.

The Black Stone is now set in the wall in a silver surround, like a big inverted bowl with an opening in the centre (see p. 24). The stone has a deep hollow in its middle, where it has been worn away by the kisses of millions of pilgrims through the ages. Muhammad himself encouraged this practice. Those pilgrims who cannot get close enough to kiss or touch it in the crowds, raise their hand to it as they pass.

There is a door into the Ka'bah, but it is rarely used, because the building has been empty since Muhammad destroyed the idols that it housed, back in 630 CE. Muhammad restored the Ka'bah to what he believed had been its original purpose: the centre for the worship of the One God.

Tawaf: the Circling

Pilgrims move around the Ka'bah in an anti-clockwise direction, seven times (preferably running the first three, and walking the last four). They start and finish counting the circuits from the corner where the Black Stone is. If at all possible, they should kiss or touch this stone, since Muhammad used to do this, or at least salute it as they go by.

The Circling demonstrates the unity of the believers in the worship of the One God, as they move in harmony together around their central shrine, each reciting an individual verse of the Qur'an.

At the end of the Circling, they go to the Station of Ibrahim to pray two *rak'ahs*.

Sa'y: the Running

There is a covered way which extends out from the Sacred Mosque, and is built between two hills, called As-Safa and Al-Marwa. Pilgrims must hurry along this passage, seven times, beginning at As-Safa which is nearest to the Sacred Mosque, and finishing at Al-Marwa. There is a corridor down the middle for those who cannot move so fast, or may be in wheelchairs; the other pilgrims pass on either side, in one direction only.

In performing this ritual, pilgrims are re-enacting Hajar's frantic search for water,

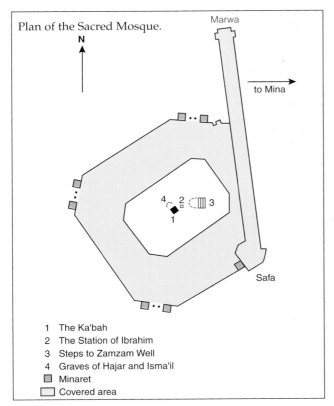

Plan of the Sacred Mosque.

N

Marwa

to Mina

Safa

1 The Ka'bah
2 The Station of Ibrahim
3 Steps to Zamzam Well
4 Graves of Hajar and Isma'il
▪ Minaret
▭ Covered area

when left in the desert with her young son Isma'il. The story tells how they were saved from dying of thirst. Isma'il dug his heels into the sand, where Hajar had left him, and a spring of water gushed up.

Pilgrims can still visit this spring, at the Zamzam Well. There are steps leading down to it, in a chamber under the courtyard of the Sacred Mosque. Many pilgrims bathe the edge of their ihram in it, and take some of the water home with them.

The Day of 'Arafat

The Plain of 'Arafat lies about 24 km east of Makkah, in hilly terrain, with the Mount of Mercy in the centre. Pilgrims must be there for the period from noon to dusk on 9 Dhul Hijja. Some gather there the previous evening, but most come on from Mina (about 10 km from Makkah) after the dawn prayer.

The most important part of the Hajj is the 'Standing before Allah' at 'Arafat, where pilgrims beg forgiveness of their sins. It is an amazing sight to see about 2 million people, out in the relentless heat of the desert, and swarming over the Mount of Mercy, engrossed in their devotions. It calls to mind for Muslims the Day of Judgement, as the following passage shows. It is from an article entitled 'Journey to Mercy'.

Witnessing this, one cannot but think of the day of Reckoning which we must all keep in mind every minute of every day. The day of Arafat is extremely difficult. How much more difficult will that day be. On the day of Arafat you beg God's mercy. On the day of Reckoning you need God's mercy. It is for that day that you must seriously consider fulfilling every pillar of the pledge as a Muslim. It is for that that you should plan to complete Hajj as soon as you are capable, for Hajj is one way you may, if Allah wills, erase all your sins, secure for yourself forgiveness and ensure Allah's mercy.

(From Islamic Cultural Centre Newsletter No. 31, *for Dhul Hijja)*

Pilgrims perform the noon and afternoon prayers together at 'Arafat, then move off at dusk to spend the night at Muzdalifah, where they perform the sunset and night prayers.

At Mina
Stoning the Devil

The next day, on 10 Dhul Hijja, the pilgrims arrive at Mina, where the 'Stoning of the Devil' takes place. On this day, they throw seven small pebbles at the pillar known as the 'Great Devil'. The ritual continues on 11 and 12 Dhul-Hijjah, when they throw seven pebbles at each of three pillars (hence 49 pebbles

Activities

Key Elements

1 Describe what the Ka'bah looks like.
2 What does the word 'ka'bah' mean?
3 The Black Stone is not the Ka'bah. What is it?
4 What name is Ibrahim known by in the Judaeo-Christian tradition?
5 Why is Ibrahim important in Islam?
6 Why do Muslims pray at the Station of Ibrahim?
7 Describe where and how the Circling takes place.
8 Describe where and how the Running takes place.
9 What story lies behind the ritual jogging between Mounts As-Safa and Al-Marwa?
10 Why is the Zamzam Well significant?

in all). Some pilgrims continue the practice into 13 Dhul Hijja (hence 70 pebbles in all).

The police are well in attendance at the pillars, since this ritual could be dangerous, if the pilgrims were to get carried away with it. A Hajj handbook gives the warning: 'What is prescribed is to be gentle and to throw the pebbles without hurting anyone.' (*A Guide to Hajj*, Umrah and Visitat to the Prophet's Mosque, pp. 50–51.)

What is the purpose of this strange ritual? There are two reasons behind it. Firstly, it reminds pilgrims of the famous story of Ibrahim and his son Isma'il, in which Allah tested their faith by asking Ibrahim to sacrifice his son to him. Three times the devil tempted Ibrahim not to do it, and tempted Isma'il to run away. But both father and son withstood the temptations, and they drove away the devil by throwing stones at him. They were prepared to go through with the sacrifice, in obedience to Allah's command, and out of love for Allah. Then, at the last moment, Allah stopped Ibrahim's hand, and provided a ram for sacrifice instead.

The other purpose and meaning of this ritual is a much more personal one. As the pilgrims 'Stone the Devil', they are expressing their own rejection of evil and their own resolve to withstand any temptations which may come their way.

The Animal Sacrifice

Pilgrims on Hajj are obliged, if they can afford it, to offer an animal for sacrifice. This is done at Mina, where the meat is roasted and enjoyed by the pilgrims, but at least a third of it must be given to those who are too poor to buy their own animal. (Since there is too much meat to distribute all at once, the Saudi government has now installed refrigeration for it, at Mina.)

'Stoning the Devil' at Mina.

This sacrifice is another reminder of the story of Ibrahim and Isma'il, since a ram was given to Ibrahim to sacrifice instead of his son. By sacrificing animals, Muslims recognise that the meat which we eat is a gift from Allah which should never be taken for granted. Also, since animals are very expensive, it is a sign that Muslims are prepared to give up things for their religion.

After making this sacrifice, pilgrims can change out of their ihram and rest for a while before putting on the ihram again and completing the rituals of the Hajj. It is at this stage in the proceedings that they have their hair cut (a woman may just have a lock of hair snipped off; a man may have his whole head shaved). This is a sign that they are coming out of the state of consecration.

Id-ul-Adha

This means the 'Major Festival', and it is also called the 'Festival of Sacrifice'. For while the pilgrims are sacrificing their animals near to the holy city of Makkah, Muslims all over the world are joining them in making an animal sacrifice: a goat or sheep per family, or a cow or camel between a larger group.

In Muslim countries, animals are usually bought a few weeks before Id and sacrificed on Id day in the backyard. In Britain, a special licence is needed to slaughter animals, which have to be stunned first. So Muslims go along to their local slaughterhouse, where the animal's throat is slit in the traditional way, with the Bismillah said over it. There is a lot of controversy in Western countries over the ritual slaughter of animals. Scientists cannot agree which method causes least pain and trauma; but Muslims believe that their method is the kindest, quickest and least painful form of death.

A third of the meat is eaten by the family which bought it; a third is given to friends and relatives; and a third given to the poor. In Western countries it may be given to an old people's home. Some Muslims in the West send money to Pakistan or India, to pay for an animal to be sacrificed there instead and given to the poor.

The meaning of this sacrifice is the same as for those on the Hajj.

* It reminds Muslims of the story of Ibrahim and Isma'il, and of their willingness to make great sacrifices for Allah.

* It shows their own readiness to make sacrifices for their religion.

* It is a way of giving thanks to the Creator God for the meat they eat.

Activities

Key Elements

1 Describe where and how the Standing takes place.
2 Why is the Day of 'Arafat compared to the Day of Judgement?
3 Describe where and how the Stoning of the Devil takes place.
4 Who was Ibrahim's son, from whom the Arabs claim to be descended?
5 What is the other English title for the Major Festival?

Think About It

6 Do you think Hajj should be made any easier for the pilgrims?
7 Why do you think forgiveness of sins is so important to people?

- It shows their concern to share their wealth with the poor.

In addition:
- It is a way for the Muslims back home to show their support for their fellow Muslims who are completing the Hajj.

Like Id-ul-Fitr, this festival is a holiday from school or work (lasting three days in Muslim countries), and begins with congregational prayers in the mosque. People dress up in their best clothes, send each other cards and gifts, and share meals with each other.

The Ummah

This photograph of pilgrims around the Ka'bah is a perfect expression of the **Ummah**, the Islamic community. It is the worldwide fellowship of Muslims which transcends race, nationality, colour, gender and language. There are many indications of this brotherhood within Islam, but nowhere is it more obvious than on the Hajj.

- The Hajj gathers together about two million people each year, for a common purpose – the largest annual gathering of people anywhere in the world, as this extract from a Muslim *Newsletter* states:

The Hajj is a unique annual conference, convened by Allah Subhanahu wa Ta'ala. He has ordained its time, prescribed its place, selected the participants and ordered its programme. . . .

Hajj should make Muslims the envy of the world, for no other nation on earth can boast or co-ordinate a conference of such magnitude every year, bringing Muslims together from all over the globe . . . to meet in unity of mind and spirit, brotherhood and understanding.

(Subhanahu wa Ta'ala means Glorified and Exalted.)

(Editorial ICC Newsletter, No. 31)

There are many other examples of Islamic fellowship.

- Muslims all over the world face the Ka'bah when they pray. It is therefore a sign of unity, as the focus of their prayers. This point is made even more strongly, when you see crowds of Muslims praying in the courtyard all round the Ka'bah, or performing the ritual Circling of the Ka'bah together.

- Whenever Muslims pray together, they stand in lines, shoulder to shoulder, to emphasise their unity with each other. And at the end of the prayers, they turn to bless their fellow Muslims on their right and on their left. At Hajj, you can see over a million pilgrims doing this at 'Arafat, when they perform the noon and afternoon prayers, standing in orderly rows and going through the prayer motions together.

- When pilgrims put on their ihram, they are all dressed alike. There is no distinction between rich or poor, king or commoner. Again, this is a sign of unity.

- When pilgrims are making the sacrifice at Mina, Muslims throughout the world are joining in the animal sacrifice.

- Their concern for their Muslim brothers and sisters who are poor is shown in the sharing of the sacrificial meat on the Hajj.

- Whether or not they come from Arabic-speaking countries, all Muslims learn the Arabic Qur'an and the Arabic words for salah (see Chapter 2). So, although the many pilgrims speak in a multitude of different languages, they can all join together in the same language for worship.

- The Islamic Empire, once known as **Dar-ul-Islam**, the 'House of Islam', no longer exists; but there is still a sense of responsibility between one Islamic state and another. It can be seen at the Hajj, when the Saudi royal house, as guardian of the sacred cities of Makkah and Madi-nah, takes a paternal role towards the pilgrims who come there from all over the world. Saudi Arabia's oil wealth has also enabled it to give aid to some of the poor Islamic countries, like Pakistan.

The importance of the Ummah is summed up in this final quotation:

Those who believe obtain their strength by believing that they are but one brotherhood. Allah Subhanahu wa Ta'ala says in the Holy Qur'an: 'Those who believe are but one single brotherhood.'

Therefore true believers feel for their brothers and sisters and they likewise for them. They should help each other wherever they are, look after each other when unwell, guard their belongings while they are away, support them in their needs especially when their lives are in danger, keep them company when they are alone, support them in their struggle for earning their livelihood. By doing so, then each individual's strength becomes the strength of all the believers.

('Friday Khutba', ICC Newsletter No. 43)

Consider what these ahadith mean:

Each of you is a mirror of his brother, if you see something wrong in your brother, you must tell him to get rid of it.

(Tirmidhi)

Believers are like the parts of a building to one another – each part supporting the others.

(Bukhari)

None of you can be a believer unless he loves for his brother what he loves for himself.

(Bukhari)

A Muslim is he from whose tongue and hands other Muslims are safe.

(Bukhari)

Vocabulary

Give the Arabic words for the following:

1 the Greater Pilgrimage
2 the Lesser Pilgrimage
3 the holiest city of Islam
4 consecration, pilgrim's clothes
5 month of pilgrimage

6 a man who has completed the Hajj
7 a woman who has completed the Hajj
8 the Major Festival
9 the Islamic community
10 the House of Islam

Assignments

1 The Hajj

a) Imagine you have just set out on the Hajj. Write a diary entry for each day of your pilgrimage, listing briefly where you went and what you did there.

b) The Hajj is now over, and you are waiting at Jeddah airport for your flight home. You get talking to a non-Muslim who asks what the Hajj is all about. Explain the purpose(s) of the Hajj as fully as possible, referring to individual parts of the Hajj where necessary.

c) You are now on the aeroplane, and have time to write a letter to your grandmother. You want to express your *feelings* about the Hajj, while they are still so vivid for you. Your grandmother is a hajja, so she will know what rituals you are referring to, so there is no need to describe them all in detail.

2 Animal Sacrifice

a) Find out all you can on what Islam teaches about the treatment of animals. (There is a section on 'Food' in Chapter 8, p. 97.)

b) Explain fully why animals are sacrificed at the Hajj and at Id-ul-Adha.

c) How far do you think Islam encourages people to respect animals?

3 Id-ul-Adha

Make a poster about Id-ul-Adha. Design it carefully so that:

a) it shows what happens at the festival;

b) it suggests the meaning(s) behind it; and

c) it expresses typical Muslim feelings about the festival.

4 The Ummah

a) Briefly summarise the examples of Muslim brotherhood given in this chapter.

b) Find as many other examples as possible, that are *not* necessarily connected with the Hajj, and explain how they demonstrate the sense of unity felt between Muslims.

c) Do you think it is possible for someone to be a good Muslim in isolation from other Muslims?

The Growth of Islam

Spread of the Islamic Empires

622–34

Muhammad had managed to unite most of Arabia under Islam. This was a remarkable achievement, considering that many of the Arabian tribes had been feuding with each other for centuries. On his death, many of these tribes broke away again. During Abu Bakr's brief caliphate of two years, he was able to suppress this revolt.

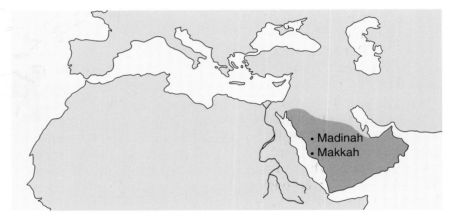

634–44

'Umar, the second caliph, took Islam beyond Arabia. First, his armies invaded Palestine, with its holy city of Jerusalem; and then they went beyond into Syria where they took the capital city, Damascus, in 635. In 642 Alexandria in Egypt was captured, and the march continued along the coast of North Africa into Libya. The following year, in the east of his empire, Isfahan in Persia (Iran) was taken.

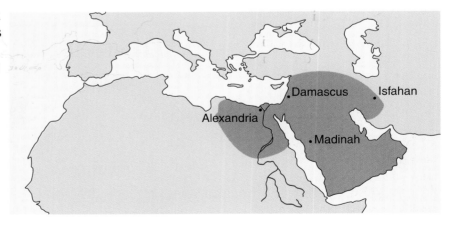

644–56

'Uthman, the third caliph, continued to push out the frontiers of the Islamic empire on all sides, reaching the borders of Afghanistan in the east.

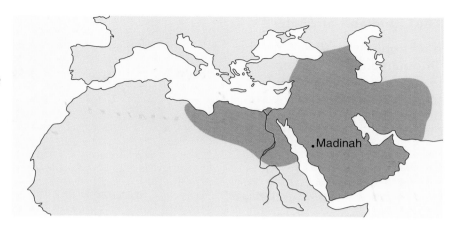

661–750

The Islamic empire continued to expand under the Umayyad Dynasty, which ruled from Damascus in Syria (and not Madinah). It reached the borders of India in the East. In 732, exactly a century after Muhammad's death, it reached its furthest point west, in France, where the Muslims were turned back at Tours by Charles Martel.

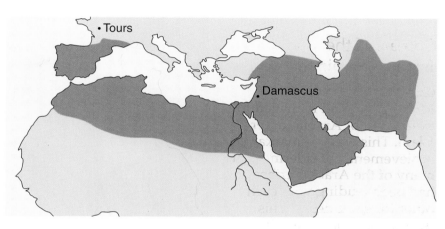

The 'Abbasid Caliphate

Some of the Umayyad caliphs were irreligious and corrupt, and they were finally overthrown (except in Spain) by the 'Abbasids who were descended from Muhammad's uncle al-'Abbas. They ruled from their new capital of Baghdad in Iraq. The 'Abbasid Dynasty was powerful for about 150 years, after which the Islamic empire was split up under a number of different dynasties.

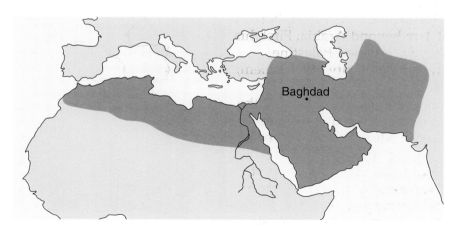

The Ottoman Caliphate

It was only with the rise of the Ottoman empire that most of the Islamic lands (except Iran, India and Central Asia) were united again. The great Ottoman empire lasted longer than any of the others, from the early sixteenth century into the twentieth century. It was ruled from Istanbul in Turkey. However, the First World War saw the break-up of the Islamic empire, and the caliphate was ended in 1924.

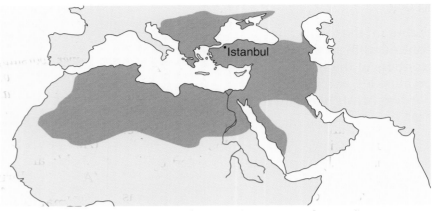

The Ottoman empire at its greatest extent, at the end of the seventeenth century CE.

Part of the Alhambra Palace, Granada, Spain. The Muslims ruled this country for seven centuries. Wherever Islam has spread, it has left a legacy of beautiful Muslim architecture, with its intricate patterns and delicately moulded stucco work.

The First Four Caliphs: the 'Rightly Guided'

Abu Bakr, the First Caliph (632–34 CE)

Muhammad had not stated clearly who should succeed him and so become caliph ('successor') and ruler of the Islamic empire. In the uncertainty following his death, Abu Bakr was hastily chosen and accepted by the majority.

There was much to commend him. He was one of Muhammad's closest friends, a Companion (see p. 27) from the very early days of Islam in Makkah. Muhammad had honoured him by marrying his daughter Ayesha. Abu Bakr belonged to the leading Quraish tribe, as had Muhammad, and was therefore more likely to be accepted by the various Arab tribesmen. He had a reputation as a good and holy man, and he continued to live humbly and in simplicity to the end of his life.

'Umar, the Second Caliph (634–44 CE)

Before Abu Bakr died in 634, he named 'Umar as his successor. 'Umar too was an early Companion of Muhammad, but in character he was very different from Abu Bakr. 'Umar was a big, strong man who had to learn to control a violent temper. There is a famous story of his conversion to Islam. He went to his sister's house to try to stop her from being a Muslim, and he even struck her, but when he read the words she had from the Qur'an he was completely won over by them. From that time onwards he became a faithful friend and supporter of the Prophet.

This account of how 'Umar and Abu Bakr reacted to Muhammad's death also shows up the difference between the two men:

> We all know what happened when the Prophet (Peace be upon him) died. At the time the Muslims found it very difficult to accept his death, they felt insecure and confused. 'Umar's immediate reaction was to angrily proclaim – 'If anyone dares to say that the Prophet (Peace be upon him) is dead, I will kill him with this sword.' Alhamdullilah, on the contrary, Abu Bakr's reac-

> tion was clear and lucid, as he said: 'If there is anyone amongst you who worshipped Muhammad, Muhammad is dead, but, whoever worshipped Allah Subhana Wa Ta'ala, Allah is always there. He is eternal.' (May Allah be pleased with them both.)

('Friday Khutba', ICC Newsletter No. 43)

(*Alhamdullilah* means 'all praise is due to Allah'; and *Allah Subhana Wa Ta'ala* means 'Allah be glorified and exalted'.)

'Umar was a great soldier, and during his reign he extended the Islamic empire beyond Arabia into Syria, Iraq and Egypt. But, for all his military power, he was a saintly man. Like Abu Bakr and Muhammad himself, he lived in simplicity, caring little for his own comfort. He was known for his good treatment of those he conquered, particularly the Jews and Christians, the 'People of the Book'.

'Uthman, the Third Caliph (644–56 CE)

'Umar appointed a council of six men to decide his successor, and they chose 'Uthman, a son-in-law of Muhammad who was from the important Umayyad family of the Quraish tribe. Although he was a deeply religious man (remembered for organising the authoritative version of the Qur'an), he proved to be a weak leader. He allowed members of his own family to take important positions in government, and was held responsible for their bad administration. He became so unpopular that he was eventually assassinated.

'Ali (656–61 CE)

The people of Madinah elected 'Ali as the next caliph. He had a strong claim to the caliphate and had waited 24 years since the Prophet's death for this honour. 'Ali was the son of Abu Talib, Muhammad's uncle and guardian. He was a lot younger than Muhammad, but had grown up in Muhammad's household, and there was a close, brotherly relationship between the two. He was the next person after Khadijah to believe in

Muhammad's prophethood, although only a boy of 10 or 12 at the time. He remained a loyal supporter of Islam ever after. At the Hijrah (see p. 27), he risked his life for Muhammad: he slept in the Prophet's bed to fool his enemies into thinking that he was still there, so giving Muhammad a head start on his pursuers. In Madinah he was a close friend and confidant of the Prophet. He married Muhammad's youngest daughter, Fatimah; and their two sons were the only surviving grandchildren of the Prophet. There are many stories which show Muhammad's fondness for these two boys.

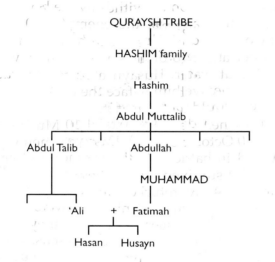

QURAYSH TRIBE
|
HASHIM family
|
Hashim
|
Abdul Muttalib
|
Abdul Talib   Abdullah
| |
'Ali + Fatimah MUHAMMAD
|
Hasan   Husayn

There are Muslims called Shi'is who believe that 'Ali was the rightful successor of Muhammad. They refuse to call him the *fourth* caliph, but the first Imam, therefore dismissing the first three caliphates as invalid. Although they look back on this period as a Golden Age, 'Ali in fact had a difficult time of it. Members of 'Uthman's family had been made governors all over the empire, and they blamed 'Ali for his death. The powerful governor of Syria, Mu'awiya, refused to recognise 'Ali as caliph until the assassins had been brought to justice.

Civil war broke out in which 'Ali proved himself a good soldier, but he eventually made peace. Some of 'Ali's followers took this as a sign of weakness, demanding that Allah alone should decide the outcome. 'Ali wasted valuable time and resources dealing with them. They became known as the Kharijites (the 'Seceders') because they were the first to withdraw formally from the other Muslims, forming a separate group within Islam. This puritanical group still exists today, but they never grew into a major movement like the Shi'i.

It is thought to have been a Kharijite who assassinated 'Ali in the mosque at Kufa, Iraq in 661. There is some question as to where his remains are buried, but the traditional site is at Najaf in Iraq, which has since become an important religious centre. Among other things, it can boast the world's largest cemetery, surrounding 'Ali's shrine. The corpses of Shi'is from all over the world are brought here, to be taken inside the sanctuary and then carried three times round the outside of 'Ali's mausoleum, before being buried near to the tombs of 'Ali and some of the other Imams.

Activities

Key Elements

1 Name the capital cities connected with the following:
   a) Muhammad
   b) the early Caliphs
   c) the Umayyad Dynasty
   d) the 'Abbasid Dynasty
   e) the Ottoman empire

2 Briefly describe the following:
   a) Abu Bakr
   b) 'Umar
   c) 'Uthman
   d) 'Ali

Shi'i Islam

The Shi'i are named after the Shi'a of 'Ali – the Party of 'Ali. They can be called Shi'is or Shi'ites; and you can talk of Shi'i Islam, Shi'ism or the Shi'a. The Shi'is have always been a minority in Islam, and today they make up about 15% of all Muslims. The largest group of Shi'is (about 48 million) is in Iran, where they form over 96% of the population. Iran is the only country to make Shi'ism the official religion. The Shi'is also form the largest religious group in Iraq. There are also Shi'i minorities in India, Pakistan, the Gulf States, the USSR and East Africa.

Virtually all of the remaining 85% of Muslims are Sunnis – those who claim to follow the right 'path' of Islam.

Hasan, the Second Imam (661–9 CE)

Shi'is regard 'Ali as the first Imam and believe that, on his death, his authority passed to his eldest son, Hasan, who became the second Imam. (The word **imam** means a leader, and it is used here by the Shi'i to denote the divinely chosen leader of their community).

By this time, Mu'awiya had extended his power so much that he forced Hasan to renounce any claims he had to the caliphate. Freed from opposition, Mu'awiya began the powerful Umayyad Dynasty which ruled the Islamic empire from Damascus in Syria for about 90 years until 750 CE. Hasan retired to Madinah where he lived quietly until his death eight years later.

Husayn, the Third Imam (669–80 CE) 'Prince of Martyrs'

After Hasan's death, his younger brother, Husayn, became head of the House of 'Ali and, according to Shi'is, the third Imam. He knew that there were supporters of the House of 'Ali in Kufa in Iraq, because there had been a revolt there in 671. The seven leaders who were executed became the first Shi'i martyrs. Husayn did nothing until Mu'awiya's death in 680. Then he set out from Arabia with a small army of 72 men, to challenge the authority of Mu'awiya's son, Yazid, at Kufa.

Despite warnings that Yazid's army had a tight hold on Kufa, Husayn pressed onwards. The first detachment of soldiers from Kufa negotiated with him, and he agreed not to march on the city. On 2 Muharram, they encamped on the Plain of Karbala. This first detachment later deserted to Husayn's side, but by this time reinforcements had arrived and cut off their water supply.

By the evening of 9 Muharram, the situation was desperate. Husayn had refused to pledge allegiance to Yazid, and had been refused permission to withdraw. He had only a small army against the enemy's 4000. He had women and children with him, including his sister and two of his sons; and they were all without water. Husayn tried to persuade his men to leave him to face the enemy alone, but they would not hear of it.

On the next day, the fateful 10 Muharram AH 61 (10 October 680 CE), Husayn's men were all killed in battle, and the women and children who survived were taken captive. The Umayyad army returned to Kufa with the heads of Husayn and his followers raised aloft on their spears. Later they took Husayn's head to Yazid in Damascus. It was returned 40 days after his death, to be buried with what remained of his body, where he fell in Karbala. A shrine to Husayn was built there and Karbala became an important religious centre. Many Shi'is have been buried there.

The massacre at Karbala has had the greatest impact in the history of Shi'ism, which gained momentum from this time. An underground resistance movement was formed in Kufa, called the Penitents – because they were sorry they had not gone to Husayn's aid. In 684 CE 3000 of them revolted and, inspired by the example of Karbala, they were killed in battle against a force of 30 000. This shows the spirit of martyrdom which was to mark the Shi'i movement.

'Ashura

The message of Karbala is that Husayn chose death rather than compromise what he believed; and the story of his self-sacrifice still moves Shi'is to tears and to acts of heroism, as it is commemorated each year. For the first ten days of the month of Muharram, the entire Shi'i world is plunged into mourning. This comes to a climax on 10 Muharram, the day of 'Ashura (which was a day of fasting long before Husayn's martyrdom). People attend emotional meetings, where Husayn's sufferings are recounted. Women break their glass bangles (usually only done when a woman's husband dies). There are also processions, when a replica corpse or coffin is carried through the streets to the sound of chants and the rhythmic beating of breasts.

Some men carry sticks or chains with which to lash their own backs until the blood flows, or swords to cut a gash in their foreheads. In Iran, Iraq and Southern Lebanon there are theatrical presentations of the tragedy at Karbala.

All these rituals keep alive the memory of Husayn and, to a lesser extent, his elder brother Hasan. They also glorify suffering and martyrdom, which has an important part to play in Shi'i Islam. Shi'is claim that all their imams died as martyrs; and the Shi'i communities have always been persecuted minorities.

An 'Ashura procession.

Shi'i Sects

In the tenth and eleventh centuries CE, Shi'ism achieved political power over almost the whole Islamic world. Then, in the eleventh century, they were severely repressed by the Turks of the Seljuk Dynasty. At the end of the fifteenth century, the Safavid Dynasty came to power in Persia (Iran) and ruled for over 200 years. They became Shi'i and made it the official religion of Persia.

The main branch of Shi'ism, the Twelvers, or Imamis, are found mostly in Iran today. Their name comes from their belief that their twelfth Imam, called Muhammad, did not die but disappeared. While they await his return, they rely on his representatives to lead them, like the Ayatollahs (meaning 'Sign of Allah').

The next largest group of Shi'is is in Lebanon and Syria, and scattered throughout Africa and Asia. They are the Seveners, or Isma'ilis, so called because they accept only seven imams and believe that their seventh Imam, called Isma'il, is the Hidden Imam. Their present leader is the Aga Khan.

A famous Sevener group of the twelfth and thirteenth centuries was known as the Assassins (or Hashishi). They doped themselves with hashish, and then committed daring acts of terrorism against Muslim statesmen.

The Seveners look for the hidden meaning of the Qur'an in even greater depth than other Shi'is, and they have given birth to a number of secretive sects, like the Druze.

The Alawi form another small Shi'i sect. Their name means 'worshippers of 'Ali'. They are found in Syria and have combined Islamic beliefs with many others from different religions.

Further Information

Some Ways in which Shi'i Islam Differs from Sunni Islam

Leadership

1   Shi'is believe that Muhammad chose 'Ali as his successor. He should therefore have been accepted by all Muslims as the first caliph – or Imam, as they call their leaders.

2   The only caliph that both Shi'is and Sunnis accept is 'Ali. In particular, Shi'is reject the caliphates of Abu Bakr, 'Umar and 'Uthman, and they do not accept any changes implemented by them. (N.B. A minority of Shi'is, the Zaydis, *do* accept the first three caliphs as well as 'Ali. These represent the most moderate form of Shi'ism.)

3   Shi'is believe that each new leader of the Muslim community should be chosen by the previous Imam, by divine inspiration (so that it is really Allah's choice). They also think he should be a descendant of Muhammad, and thus of 'Ali.

4   The Sunni caliphs held mainly political power. For the Shi'is, their leader's religious authority was far more important. (They could therefore regard Hasan as their Imam, even when he had no political influence.)

The Scriptures

5   Sunnis believe that Muhammad's role in revealing Allah's laws (in the Qur'an) and guiding people to Allah (in the Sunnah) ended with him. Shi'is cannot believe that Allah would ever leave them without guidance, and that their leaders have the right to interpret the Qur'an for them. It follows that their Imams must be sinless and unable to make mistakes because Allah would not lead his people astray.

6   Sunnis interpret the Qur'an literally, but Shi'is claim that its hidden meaning was given by Muhammad to 'Ali.

7   Sunnis accept six books of Hadith which they call 'The Accurate Six'. Shi'is have their own collection of books of Hadith, mostly passed on through the Imams.

Beliefs

8 The Shi'is expect the **Madhi** (the divinely 'guided' one) to appear before the Day of Judgement, and bring in a reign of justice and peace. This is a popular belief among Sunnis as well; but the Shi'is expect the Mahdi to be their Hidden Imam (i.e. their last Imam, whom they believe to have disappeared rather than died).

Ritual Practices

9 All Muslims accept the Five Pillars, but Shi'is are permitted to combine the five prayers into three sessions.

10 Shi'is have many saints. The Twelvers, for instance, venerate the Fourteen Pure Ones (Muhammad, his daughter Fatimah and the Twelve Imams). They perform elaborate rituals at their shrines, and commemorate their births and deaths annually.

Sufism

The Sufis are Muslims who are not content with *doing* the Five Pillars; they also want to *feel* as close to Allah as possible. They live simple lives, devoting their time and energy to deepening their relationship with Allah. The rough woollen robes which some of them used to wear may have given the name 'Sufism' to this movement in Islam, because *suf* means 'wool'. It was thought that some of the early followers of the Prophet wore simple clothes like this. Sufis look back on the first four caliphs in particular as saintly men who led simple lives, close to Allah; and they try to follow their examples.

The Whirling Dervishes

The early Sufis were individuals who devoted their lives to meditating on the Qur'an. Since the twelfth and thirteenth centuries CE, they have been organised into Orders, or Brotherhoods, led by Shayks who have handed down their secret teachings to their pupils. Sufis claim that these chains of authority go back to Muhammad himself. Each Order teaches its own path (**tariqah**), or method of tuning in to Allah. This may be through silent meditation done to rhythmic breathing, or through rhythmic chanting, or dance. The most famous method is that of the Mevlevi in Turkey, known as the Dancing or Whirling Dervishes. In a sacred dance, each dervish spins round and round on the spot, with one hand raised to heaven and the other pointing down to the earth, trying to become a channel of communication between the two. Their dancing is carefully controlled, and when the music stops, they form up and file out in an orderly way. (Most Muslims, however, reject dancing and music in their religion.)

The Conference of the Birds

Sufi teachings are often difficult to understand, because the idea is that they should be experienced rather than just studied (just as you can read about love, but you will never fully understand it until you are in love). Sufis often put across their ideas in stories, because the listener can enter imaginatively into the story and experience something of its meaning. A famous Sufi story from the twelfth century CE is the Conference of the Birds. It tells how birds were called to undertake a long and hazardous journey to find the king bird. Not all of them responded to the call, and many disappeared on the way as they met with difficulties and dangers. Only 30 managed to complete the journey and reach their king. When they did, they discovered that they were no longer 30 separate birds, but they were all part of the king bird. This story has a deep meaning: the king bird represents Allah, and the journey is the spiritual journey each person is called to make in life.

Al-Ghazali (1059–111 CE)

Al-Ghazali was one of the greatest scholars of Islam, and he helped to make Sufism accept-

Whirling Dervishes in Damascus, Syria.

able within Islam. He was a brilliant professor in Baghdad until his late thirties, when he became more and more dissatisfied with intellectual knowledge alone. So he tried Sufism, which had a great influence on his later writings. He taught that the external practices of religion need to go hand-in-hand with personal, inner religious faith. He thought that Sufism was one way of approaching Allah, but he rejected its claim to have special, hidden truth of its own.

Sufism has sometimes met with disapproval and opposition, but more often it has been tolerated and recognised as a valid part of Islam. Today, Sufism is found not only in the Sufi Orders but also in its more general influence on popular religious worship. One example of this is **dhikr**, the 'remembrance' of Allah through the repetition of his name. Phrases like *Allahu Akbar* and *La ilaha illallah* are frequently on Muslims' lips; and others such as *Subhanallah*, which means 'Glory be to Allah', and *Al hamdu lilla*, which means 'All praise be to Allah'. The use of prayer-beads to count off the number of repetitions also comes from Sufism. Muslims believe that dhikr will bring them closer to Allah and help them to keep his commandments.

Further Information

Some Sufi Writings

These two extracts are taken from *Alive to God, Muslim and Christian Prayer* by Kenneth Cragg (pp. 81 and 92). The first is a poem by an Egyptian Sufi master of the thirteenth century CE:

My God and my Lord, eyes are at rest, stars are setting, hushed
are the movements of birds in their nests, of monsters in the deep. [. . .]

The doors are locked, watched by their bodyguards.
But thy door is open to him who calls on thee.
My Lord, each lover is now alone with his beloved.
Thou for me art the beloved One.

('Abd al-'Aziz al-Dirini; Purity of Heart)

A Sufi Muslim in Kenya praying at the tomb of the great teacher Habib Salih.

The following is from a prayer of the Naqsha-bandi Order of Sufis, which was founded in Persia in the fourteenth century CE by Baha' al-Din Naqshabandi:

O my God, how gentle art thou with him who has transgressed against thee: how near thou art to him who seeks thee, how tender to him who petitions thee, how kindly to him who hopes in thee.

Who is he who asked of thee and thou didst deny him, or who sought refuge in thee and thou didst betray him, or drew near to thee and thou didst hold him aloof, or fled unto thee and thou didst repulse him?

Questions

- In the poem, how does al-Dirini think of God?

- Pick out the four words in the opening part of the prayer by Naqshabandi which describe God.

Activities

Key Elements

1 Explain the meaning of the name 'Sunni'.
2 Explain how Shi'ism got its name.
3 Who was the only caliph accepted by both Sunnis and Shi'is?
4 Why do Shi'is want to be buried at Najaf and Karbala?
5 What does the festival of 'Ashura commemorate?
6 Why did the Shi'i line of imams come to an end?
7 What are the two main Shi'ite sects?

Think About It

8 Do you admire people who believe in something so strongly that they are prepared to die for it? (Try to think of actual examples.)
9 Is there anything that you would die for?
10 What do you think is the meaning of the Sufi story of the Conference of the Birds?

The Muslim World Today

The maps over the page show that Muslims are now spread throughout the world; but most are still found in the traditional Muslim countries to which Islam originally spread from Arabia. In 1983 the Muslim Educational Trust claimed that there were over 42 Muslim countries (the smaller Gulf States, for example, are not shown on Map B). The total world population of Muslims is estimated at about 800 million; although some Muslim sources claim that it is as much as 1000 million.

The country with the greatest number of Muslims is Indonesia in South Asia with over 160 million, followed by Pakistan with over 130 million. Although only about 12% of the population of India are Muslims, there are about 125 million Muslims there (it is a large, densely populated country).

The three biggest Muslim countries in terms of land mass are Sudan, Algeria and Saudi Arabia. Each of these is about the size of all the European countries put together (but they have large stretches of desert and are therefore sparsely populated).

Of all the Muslim countries, Turkey has done most to Westernise its laws. At the other extreme, Saudi Arabia, Pakistan and Iran have strictly adhered to Shari'ah laws and applied them most widely. Iran is the only country to make Shi'i Islam the state religion.

(To check on population figures and Muslim percentages of any country, you can ask in the Reference Section of your local library for the current edition of *The Statesman's Year-Book*, published by Macmillan.)

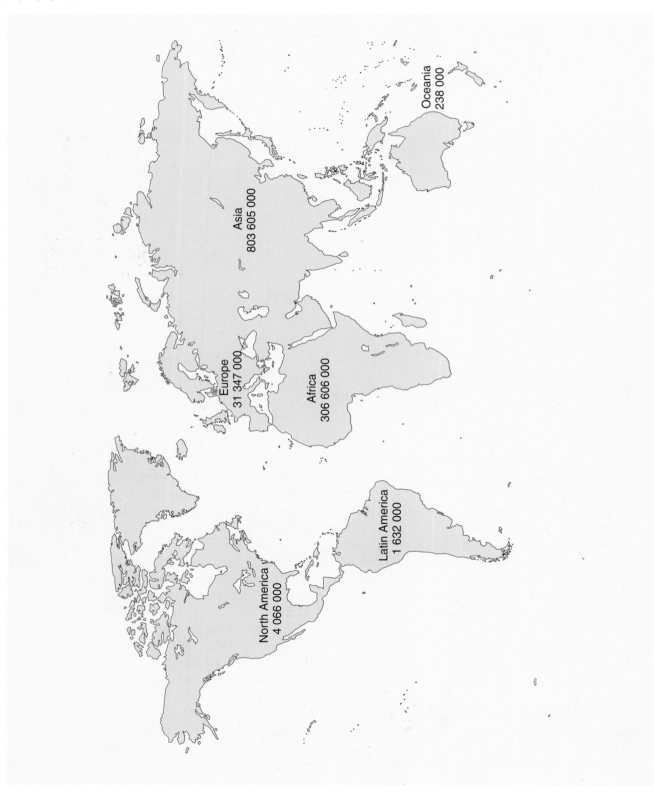

Map A:
World distribution
of Islam by six
continental areas,
mid-1997. (Figures,
to the nearest
thousand, are
taken from *World
Christian
Encyclopedia*, Second
Edition, OUP.)

North America
4 066 000

Latin America
1 632 000

Europe
31 347 000

Africa
306 606 000

Asia
803 605 000

Oceania
238 000

Map B:
The Muslim world.

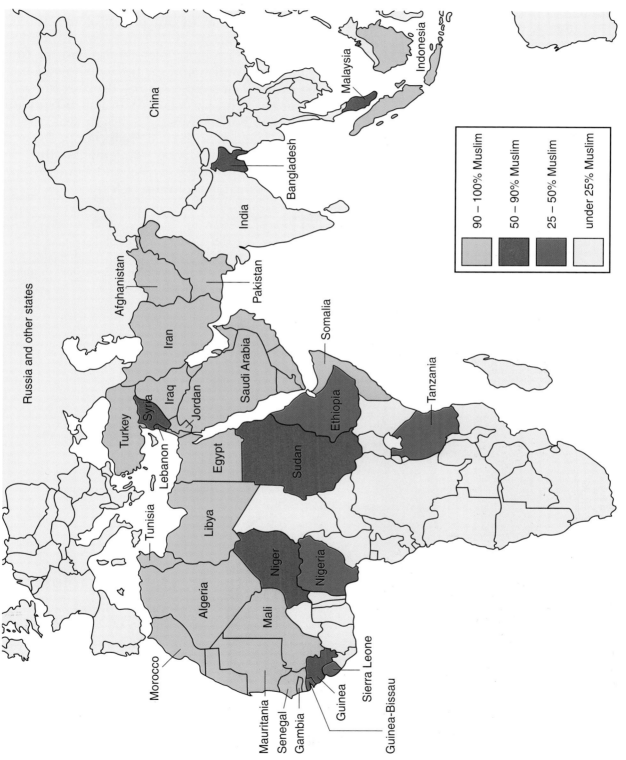

Legend:
- 90 – 100% Muslim
- 50 – 90% Muslim
- 25 – 50% Muslim
- under 25% Muslim

Country labels: China, Malaysia, Indonesia, Bangladesh, India, Afghanistan, Pakistan, Russia and other states, Iran, Somalia, Saudi Arabia, Tanzania, Turkey, Syria, Iraq, Jordan, Ethiopia, Lebanon, Egypt, Sudan, Tunisia, Libya, Niger, Nigeria, Algeria, Mali, Morocco, Mauritania, Senegal, Gambia, Guinea, Sierra Leone, Guinea-Bissau

Iran

From the early twentieth century, there was a struggle between the religious leaders, called the 'ulama, and the Shah, the head of state in Iran. The 'ulama, representing the conservative element, wanted the country to follow Shari'ah laws (Islamic law based on the Qur'an and the Sunnah) and they wanted to be in charge of administering it and guiding the community.

The Shahs, concerned for their own power, and in an attempt to bring Iran into the modern secular world, tried to reduce the influence of the 'ulama. The state gradually took control of education, the law-courts and social services. Westernisation was encouraged, with women forbidden to wear the veil, and the lunar calendar changed to a solar one. But the Shahs were unable to affect the deeply ingrained religious conservatism of the country and the popular respect for the 'ulama.

In 1963 the most outspoken of the 'ulama won the support of the masses. As a high ranking Shi'i religious leader, he had the title Ayatollah; and his black turban showed that he claimed descent from the Prophet himself, through 'Ali. He was Ayatollah Khomeini 1902–89). For the next 14 years he was forced to live in exile, as the last Shah clamped down heavily on opposition movements. But, in exile, he continued to write, and from 1970 he began to incite revolution in Iran.

A roadside sign in south Beirut proclaims popular support for Ayatollah Khomeini.

The Iranian Revolution

Everything flared up in August 1977, when there began a series of demonstrations in which the police opened fire and killed large numbers of people. This only encouraged more people to seek martyrdom in what they regarded as a 'holy war' against the corruption of the Shah's regime. The Shi'i mentality created a new Karbala: the Iranians saw themselves in the role of Husayn's followers against the mighty forces of the Umayyad Dynasty. The various opposition groups united under Khomeini's banner, and the downfall of the Shah came very quickly. In January 1979 the Shah was forced to leave Iran for America (his closest Western ally); and on 1 February Khomeini returned in triumph, welcomed by a crowd of two million.

Khomeini became ruler and appointed the Revolutionary Council. Radical reforms were imposed, to get rid of all Western influences, and to set up an Islamic Republic. Not everyone was happy with these measures, nor with the severity with which the local Revolutionary Committees often carried them out. But Khomeini retained much popular support and continued as leader for ten years, until his death. The mosque is now the centre of social life; the Friday prayer is a major weekly event, and the sermon used for political messages (often government announcements). Women are once more veiled and polygamy is legal again, allowing men up to four wives.

The Gulf War (1980–88)

Iran's internal affairs were overshadowed in the international news by the outbreak of its war with Iraq. These two countries are traditional enemies: Iraq being an Arab country, and Iran Persian. Besides which, there have always been fears that Iran would try to annex the area in the south of Iraq where the holiest Shi'i shrines of Karbala and Najaf are situated. Although Iraq started the Gulf War, Khomeini had been inciting the Shi'is of Iraq to rebellion, which, as they account for over half the population, was seen as a serious threat. In 1988, after a prolonged and crippling war, during which hundreds of thousands of young men (and even Iranian boys) died on the battle fields of Iraq, Khomeini finally agreed to accept the United Nations' proposals for a ceasefire.

Saudi Arabia
The Wahhabis

The Arabian House of Saud has been associated with the Wahhabi Islamic movement since it began with 'Abd-al-Wahhab in the eighteenth century CE. He preached a return to the **Shari'ah**, i.e. laws based on the Qur'an and the Sunnah. The Wahhabis are puritanical, in that they disapprove of all frivolity like music, dancing and the wearing of gold by men; they are highly moral and live simple lives. They are opposed to any mixing of the sexes in public (even shaking hands), and would prefer women to stay in the confines of their homes. In religious practices, they emphasise the oneness of Allah above all else and are therefore strongly against the veneration of saints and the building of their shrines. Their mosques are plain and simple.

The House of Saud

The House of Saud unified Arabia in the Kingdom of Saudi Arabia in 1932. This was on the wave of Wahhabi revival, so we should expect to find Islam strictly enforced there. The King is both the political and religious leader but, although he is individually very powerful, he must act within the Shari'ah (the Islamic law), if he wishes to retain his support. In 1964, for example, King Saud was forced to abdicate by the 'People Who Bind and Loose', an organisation of senior princes, 'ulama notables, and government leaders who safeguard the Shari'ah.

The two holiest sites of Islam are situated in Saudi Arabia – at Makkah and Madinah. The King is the guardian of these sites and his government accommodates the millions of pilgrims who come there from all over the world. He is therefore an important leader for the Islamic world, as well as for Saudi Arabia, and has given foreign aid to poorer Islamic states like Pakistan and to Muslim communities abroad.

Oil revenue has plunged Saudi Arabia into the modern technological revolution (particularly since 1970, when oil prices began to rise

The modern city of Riyadh.

dramatically). Oil production meant that the country needed a skilled and educated workforce, and its revenue provided the money for development. The monarch has had to lead his country into modernisation, without betraying its basic Islamic principles. He constantly runs the risk of going too slowly for the new middle class of graduate city-dwellers; and of going too fast for the traditionalists. The seizure of the Sacred Mosque by an extremist Islamic group in 1979 was just one sign of this danger.

Saudi Arabia is therefore a curious mixture of the ancient and the modern. Its capital city, Riyadh, has impressive modern buildings spreading out beyond what remains of the old mud-walled city. Education now includes more secular than religious subjects; but modern radio and television are used for a lot of religious education. Girls now make up about half the primary and secondary school population; but there is strict segregation of the sexes at all levels. Some women go on to higher education; but they have to be taken to

and from college by a male member of their family, since women are forbidden to drive or travel alone. Women are now allowed to appear on television, to read the news and present children's programmes – as long as they are not Saudi women.

So Saudi Arabia is making use of Western technology to serve its own purposes, within an Islamic framework.

The Indian Subcontinent

Islam was first established in India (which is traditionally Hindu) early in the eighth century; but it took a strong hold there from the sixteenth to eighteenth centuries, under the Mughal Dynasty. The Mughals invaded India from the north-west and gradually spread further south, to rule almost the entire sub-continent; but their influence remained strongest in the north.

Apart from Akbar, the Mughal emperors tended to see it as their duty to convert people to Islam by force if necessary, and to stamp out other religions. Islam's hatred of idolatry resulted in the destruction of many beautiful temples and images, particularly in northern India. Those who resisted Islam were persecuted; but some were attracted to it. These tended to be the outcasts, at the bottom of Hindu society, who had most to gain from the message of equality in Islam. The intolerance shown by the Mughal rulers created a history of bitterness between these two religions in India, which could break out in atrocities at any time, and continues to do so even today.

From the early eighteenth century, the Mughal empire began to break up into many independent princedoms. The next power to unite this vast subcontinent was Britain, which had been gaining territory there since the seventeenth century through its East India trading company. By the mid-nineteenth century it had brought hundreds of princedoms into the British Empire.

This period also saw the rise of nationalism, and in 1885 the All-India National Congress party was formed. But it was felt that this represented Hindus and, in 1906, the All India Muslim League was founded in response to Congress, to protect the interests of Muslims, who formed 21% of the Indian population.

Both parties wanted independence from Britain, but it took many more years of struggle and strife between the Hindus and Muslims before Independence was finally granted in 1947. With it came partition. The Muslim-dominated areas in the north-west and northeast were separated off from the rest of India, to form a new Muslim state called Pakistan ('Pure Homeland'). There were, of course, Hindus left in the Muslim areas and Muslims left in India, many of whom decided to move, causing huge refugee problems in both countries.

Mohammad Ali Jinnah, who had been the leader of the Muslim League and founder of Pakistan, became its first president. Unfortunately, he died soon afterwards, leaving his new country with many problems. Since 1947, Pakistan has had three major wars with India (1947–8; 1965; 1971), some civil unrest,

Although many Hindu temples were destroyed, the Mughals left behind them in India some beautiful Muslim architecture. The famous Taj-Mahal was built by Shah Jahan, the grandson of Emperor Akbar, in memory of his wife.

Mosque in Chitral, Northern Pakistan.

and three military coups. In 1971, its large eastern territory (over 1500 km away) broke away under the leadership of Sheikh Mujibur Rahman, to form the independent Muslim state of Bangladesh.

General Bhutto came to power in 1970, and tried to Westernise the country and deal with some of its pressing social problems by following a socialist policy. But the loss of Bangladesh was a severe blow to Pakistan's self-esteem, and people began to look once more to Islam for their identity. By 1977 there was an anti-Bhutto movement which criticised him for failing to further the cause of Islam. Bhutto tried to respond to the mood of the people by putting through some minor Islamic reforms. For instance, he outlawed gambling, alcohol and horse-racing, and changed the weekly holiday from Sunday to Friday. But these reforms came too late; he

was overthrown by General Zia ul-Haq, and executed the following year on a murder charge.

Zia imposed martial law in Pakistan from 1977 to 1985, and still held a tight grip on the country right up to his death in a plane crash in 1988. Being a strict Muslim, he soon set about introducing an Islamic system of laws in Pakistan. For instance, severe penalties like flogging and execution were imposed for major crimes such as rape and murder; fasting during Ramadan was strictly observed; and government offices were closed at prayer-times.

Democratic elections were held in Pakistan in November 1988. Benazir Bhutto, leader of the Pakistan People's Party, and daughter of the late President Bhutto, became Prime Minister. A firm Muslim, with an international education at Oxford and Harvard Universities, she became the first woman to run a Muslim state.

Activities

Key Elements

1 List all the Muslim countries named in this last part of the chapter on 'The Muslim World Today'. Make sure you know where these countries are.
2 Which three countries follow the Shari'ah most closely?
3 Which is the only country to have made Shi'i Islam the state religion?
4 Explain why the Shah of Iran was deposed.

5 Which Islamic school of thought has most influenced the state religion of Saudi Arabia?
6 Explain why Saudi Arabia is important for the Islamic world.
7 Name the two Islamic countries in the Indian Subcontinent.

Think About It

8 Do you think Westernisation can be a help or hindrance to Muslim countries?

9 What difficulties are faced by Muslims living in non-Muslim countries?

Vocabulary

Give the Arabic words for the following:

1 'successor' to Muhammad
2 Muslims who claim to follow the right 'path'
3 Muslims who belong to the 'party' of 'Ali
4 month in which Husayn's martyrdom is commemorated
5 name for the leader of the Shi'i community

6 name for 'the guided one' who is expected to appear
7 a title meaning 'sign of Allah'
8 wool
9 Islamic law
10 religious lawyers

Assignments

1 Shi'ism

a) *Either* by story *or* picture-strip, record the martyrdom of Husayn.

b) Explain the significance of the rituals of 'Ashura.

c) How important do you think Husayn's martyrdom is for Shi'i Muslims?

2 Sufism

a) Do some further research on Sufism, and make notes. (You might try to find some more Sufi stories or poems.)

b) Explain what Sufis are trying to achieve through their various 'paths'.

c) Why do you think Sufism has been a popular influence in Islam?

3 A Muslim Country Today

a) Choose a Muslim country to research. Write to its embassy for information, asking particularly about the role of Islam there. Present your information in a travel brochure.

b) Write a list of ten questions, the answers to which would give you explanations about the importance and influence of Islam in the country you have chosen. (You do not need to give the answers!)

c) How important do you think it is for Muslims to live in a country with Islamic laws? (Shari'ah should guide a Muslim's personal life, anyway.)

8

Growing Up in Islam

Birth Rituals

The Call to Prayer

Description: When a Muslim baby is born, his father, another man of the family, or the local imam, speaks the call to prayer into the baby's ears. The adhan is spoken into the right ear, and the 'iqamah (see p. 13) into the left. This is done as soon as possible after birth.

Meaning: Although the child cannot yet understand these words, the ceremony introduces the child to its religion and shows that the parents want to bring it up within Islam.

Muslims believe that, by following Islam, they are living in the way God intended us all to live. Islam teaches that all of us are born Muslims, because we naturally 'submit' to God's laws. They believe, therefore, that all who die in childhood will enjoy the rewards of Muslims in heaven, since it is only as we grow up that we can cease to be Muslims,

either by ignoring God or by choosing to follow another religion. Muslims therefore place great importance on encouraging their children to continue within Islam.

Aqiqah

This usually takes place when the baby is seven days old. Passages from the Qur'an are recited, and there are a number of special rituals performed.

a) Shaving the head

Description: The baby's hair is shaved off and weighed. Traditionally, its weight in gold or silver is given to the poor. Today, parents usually give a donation of whatever they can afford to charity.

Meaning: In many cultures, hair is regarded as unclean. Shaving off the hair is therefore a symbol of purity.

be known by a second name, to save the confusion of so many boys having the same name. Another tradition is to give boys one of the 99 names of Allah from the Qur'an, such as Halim which means 'patient'. When this is done, it always has the word *'Abd* in front of it, which means 'servant' (e.g. 'Abd al-Halim). In the same way, they would never call anyone Allah, but Abdullah is a common Muslim name, meaning 'Servant of Allah'.

The child is regarded as a gift and blessing from Allah. One way of saying 'Thank you' for this most precious gift is to give something in return – to be used by those who need it most.

b) Naming

Description: The child is then named. Customs vary as to who in the family is given the privilege of choosing the name: often it is the grandfather, or simply the parents.

Meaning: Names are usually chosen to honour great Muslims from the past. So a boy might be named after the Prophet Ibrahim, or the Caliph 'Umar. A girl might be named after Muhammad's wife Ayesha, or his daughter Fatimah. Many boys are given the name Muhammad, although they might well

c) Animal sacrifice

Description: It is traditional to sacrifice two sheep or goats for a boy, and one for a girl. Like the sacrifice at Id ul Adha, this is done by a halal butcher in Western countries, and a third of the meat is eaten, another third given to friends and relatives, and another third given to the poor.

Meaning: People share food together to celebrate happy occasions, providing the best food that they can afford. At all Muslim festivals, people want to share their good fortune with those who are less fortunate in life.

Although Muhammad did much to improve the situation of women, men continued to take a dominant role in Muslim society. Therefore there is particular rejoicing over the birth of a boy.

Circumcision (*Khitan*)

Description: Boys are circumcised in Islam (as in Judaism). This is often done at the Aqiqah ceremony, or at 21 days, or even when the child is older. A Muslim doctor performs the simple operation (cutting off the foreskin), after a prayer is said.

Meaning: Muslims continue to do this today because it is a religious practice which was started by the Prophet Ibrahim.

You may come across many birth customs among Muslim families other than those described here. Sometimes they have come from other cultures rather than from Islamic teachings. A few of the customs are superstitious and are frowned upon by some Muslims. One example is the tying of a black thread around the baby's wrist to ward off the Evil Eye. Other customs express the common human desire to mark special stages in the baby's life, like the first time it eats solid food, and its first birthday.

Education

Just as it is important for Muslim parents to set their children off on the right road, at birth, so it is important to continue to bring them up in the Islamic faith.

The Shari'ah

A Muslim's whole life is governed by **Shar'ah**, the Islamic law, which literally means the 'straight path'. Muslims must therefore know what is obligatory (**fard**), for example, the Five Pillars; what is permitted (**halal**); and what is forbidden (**haram**) to them.

The Shari'ah is based on the Qur'an and the Sunnah; so children will gradually learn to read the Qur'an, and will be told stories about Muhammad, as examples for them to follow.

The Shari'ah is arrived at by the common consent (**ijma'**) of Islamic scholars. Where neither the Qur'an nor the Sunnah give direct rules, the method of analogy is used. Scholars find a similar issue on which there is some teaching and apply the same principle to the new situation. For example, the killing of infants is forbidden in the Qur'an so now abortion is forbidden.

The Shari'ah encompasses both public and private life. It has laws which you would expect to be made by the political authorities, as well as rules for areas of life which might be regarded as private morality. It teaches Muslims how Allah wants them to live the whole of their lives.

Coming of Age

Some Muslim countries have Arabic as their language, but if this is not the case, it is important for Muslim children to become familiar with the Arabic that is used in their worship. The first phrase they learn is the **Bismillah**: *Bismillah ir Rahman ir Rahim* (In the name of Allah, the Compassionate, the Merciful). This is the opening of all but one of the surahs in the Qur'an, and is frequently used by Muslims. Some Muslims have a special celebration, with presents, when a child can recite it. This may be part of the child's fourth birthday celebrations, if the family remember birthdays (which is not done in every culture).

From then on, children will attend the **madrasah**. This is a religious school run by the mosque. In Islamic countries, it could be an ordinary day-school. In Western countries it is run after day-school or sometimes during the weekend. Children are taught Islamic beliefs, how to pray, and how to read the Qur'an.

There is no set time laid down in the Qur'an for coming of age in Islam. Nor is there a special ceremony for this. Muslim children will gradually learn their religion through practice, as they grow up. By about the age of seven, they will be doing the five daily prayers. By ten, they will probably be doing some daily fasts, but not yet for the whole month of Ramadan. By the time they have reached puberty, they must accept the obligations of the Five Pillars, if they are to continue to be Muslims. Some Muslim countries count this as the age of 12. At about this age, a Muslim child usually finishes learning to recite the Qur'an, and the family celebrate this event.

'Amr bin Shu'aib narrated on the authority of his father who narrated from his father that the Messenger of Allah (peace and blessing of Allah be upon him) said: Command your children to offer prayer when they attain the age of seven, and when they attain the age of ten and do not observe prayer, then force them to do so. And separate them in their beds.

(Sunan Abu Dawud; Selection from Hadith, No. 17, p. 11)

Schooling

Since Islam affects all aspects of life, there is a lot to learn, but it is picked up gradually at home and at school. This means that schooling is very important. In Islamic countries, the madrasahs teach and practise the Islamic religion. As boys and girls reach secondary level, they are segregated and are taught by teachers of their own gender.

There is naturally much concern about the education of Muslim children living in the West. Most go to ordinary local schools where they hope that their beliefs will be respected. Muslims are particularly worried about such things as the provision of halal meat at school dinners; permission for Muslim girls to wear traditional dress (e.g., loose trousers to cover their legs); and separate PE and swimming lessons for boys and girls.

Many Muslims would prefer their children to be educated in special Islamic schools. These are private schools; but Muslims in Britain had been asking for government aid (like church schools). After more than ten years, the first two Islamic primary schools were finally granted this in January 1998.

Dr Baig, headmaster of the Islamic Primary School in Brent (West of London), explains how Islamic schools are special:

'We want to educate the children with a thorough understanding of the Islamic faith and its importance, and to this end we use part of every day to teach Islamic studies. But we are also concerned with creating an atmosphere, a way of behaving which is in line with the restraint, the respect for elders, the obedience which is something Muslims believe to be very important.'

(The Times Educational Supplement)

Some people think this will increase the isolation of the Muslim community in Britain; and that we can only break down the barriers of suspicion, ignorance and intolerance by learning to live together.

This is the letter-heading of an Islamic organisation which wants to help Muslim children in non-Muslim schools.

IN THE NAME OF ALLAH THE BENEFICENT THE MERCIFUL

MECC
Muslim Education Co-ordinating Council UK

49 Kilmartin Avenue
London SW16 4RA
Tel: 0181-679 1933
Chairman: Nazar Mustafa
Secretary: Mrs Foqia Hyee

Way of Life

Food

Muslims must only eat *halal* food (which means 'permitted' according to Islamic laws, as opposed to *haram* which means 'forbidden'). All fish and vegetables are permitted, alcohol is forbidden, and there are some restrictions on meat.

Muslims are forbidden to eat any product from the pig. They are also forbidden to eat the meat of any animals which have died (and not been slaughtered). Other animals must be killed according to Islamic regulations before their meat is permitted. The animal's throat must be cut swiftly with a sharp knife, and the Bismillah blessing said over it. Muslims believe this is the most painless way of killing an animal, and it allows the blood to drain away.

Muslims are taught not to waste their food because it comes from Allah the Creator. They should take only as much food as they can eat. At the end of a meal, if there are leftovers which cannot be re-used, they are thrown out for the birds rather than being wasted.

Dress

There is much emphasis in Islam on respect for the opposite sex, and particularly on the protection of women from men's sexual desires. So Muslim society does not approve of nudity, and as children grow up they are taught to be discreet about their bodies. Once boys reach puberty, they must cover themselves at least from the navel to the knees. Girls must cover their tops as well, but do not have to cover their heads, necks and arms when they are at home or in all-female company.

Muslims gathered outside the London Central Mosque at Id-ul-Fitr, showing a variety of dress.

Outside the home, Muslim women usually cover up much more than this, depending on what is acceptable in the societies where they live. Modesty is the main consideration in dress for both sexes. Women should wear loose clothing that does not show off their figures, and the material should be thick enough not to be seen through. Women will also cover their hair and sometimes parts of their face. In strict Islamic countries, like Saudi Arabia, Pakistan and Iran, women must be fully veiled from head to toe. It is mostly a matter of the interpretation of Qur'anic passages like these:

Tell believing women to avert their glances and guard their private parts, and not to display their charms except what (normally) appears of them.

(Qur'an 24:30)

Remain in your homes and do not (publicly) display your beauty in the way they used to do during (the time of) primitive ignorance.

(Qur'an 33:33)

(The Qur'an. Basic Teachings, p. 206)

There is a lot of misunderstanding between Muslims and non-Muslim Westerners over the purpose of Islamic dress regulations. Yet it seems that most Muslims, both men and women, are in favour of Islamic dress because it gives women respect. The Chairman of The Islamic Society for the Promotion of Religious Tolerance in the UK says this:

Protected in her own symbol of dignity (her dress) the woman can feel free to take whichever role in her society that she wishes to do, without the added burden of having to constantly look beautiful (more artificially than naturally) or having to succumb to the temptation of being used for ornamental beautification of streets and offices.

The unspoken 'jargon' of the Moslem dress is really to say to the man: 'Hey, stop looking at my own private body and look at my mind instead!'

(Hesham El Essawy, letter of 25th September 1984)

Apart from modesty, another consideration is simplicity. Muslims are generally against

Activities

Key Elements

1 Why is the call to prayer spoken to the newborn baby in Islam?

2 What are the **Aqiqah** rituals?

3 On which two authorities is the Shari'ah based?

4 Write out the English translation of the Bismillah.

5 When do Muslim children 'come of age' in their religion?

6 If you wanted to serve meat to a Muslim, what would you have to consider?

7 List ten foods which would be forbidden to Muslims because they come from the pig (remember that lard, made from pork fat, is used in many food products).

8 Why do Muslims disapprove of wasting food?

9 Modesty is one of the principles behind Muslim dress regulations. What is another main principle?

10 Why should Muslim women not wear tight or see-through clothes?

Think About It

11 How far do you think parents have a right to bring up their children in their religion?

wearing clothes which show off their wealth. Nor are women allowed to wear male dress or vice versa, because of the sexual deviancy that this implies. Men are forbidden to wear silk and pure gold.

Married Life

Sex

While boys are allowed to play out on the streets, a closer eye is kept on Muslim girls. Once they reach puberty, boys and girls are not allowed to mix freely together outside their homes. This means that Western-style teenage parties and clubs are frowned upon; and Muslim girls will tend to make their own social life within their homes. Obviously, this is done to prevent promiscuity. Islam teaches that the right and only place for sex is within marriage. This does not mean that Islam is against sex. On the contrary, it regards sex as a natural part of being human and therefore as a gift from Allah. But, if people are to benefit from sex, it must be used in the way Allah intended, and not abused. So Muslims are encouraged to marry young.

Arranged Marriage

Marriages are generally arranged in Muslim communities (as is the case for two-thirds of the people of the world), although this is not laid down in the Qur'an, and no one should be forced into marrying against his or her will. A boy's parents will look out for a suitable partner for their son, and will approach the girl's parents before she is asked for her consent.

Reasons can be put forward both for and against arranged marriages, but most people seem to prefer whatever is the accepted social norm. Generally, difficulties only arise where there are conflicting ideas within society. Some Muslims growing up in the West, for instance, may be envious of their Western teenage friends who have the freedom to go out with the opposite sex and to marry whomever they want. But here is the other point of view:

It is not always harmful for the young to benefit from the experience of their loving parents, who usually look for compatible partners rather than the short-lived romantic ones. . . .

Some western girls, incidentally, confess to being secretly envious of arranged marriages as at least it lessens the risk of growing old in loneliness, as well as freeing them from having to kiss so many frogs before they find a prince!

(Hesham El Essawy, letter of 30 October 1984)

In arranged marriages, the couple have to grow to love the one they marry, rather than marry the one they love, but this still produces loving relationships which are often more stable than their Western counterparts. The tenderness and love experienced between husband and wife are seen as part of Allah's intentions for men and women, as this passage from the Qur'an shows:

And of His signs
is that He created for you, of yourselves, spouses, that you might repose in them, and He has set between you love and mercy,

(Arberry)   (Qur'an 30:20)

Part of the arrangements includes coming to an agreement about the dowry, called the **mahr**. This is a sum of money paid by the bridegroom to the bride, as a token of his appreciation of her. Officially it belongs to the wife to do with as she pleases. In practice it is often paid before the marriage to help towards the wedding expenses and setting up the newly-weds in their home. It is sometimes paid partly in goods. There is another delayed dowry, the amount of which is stated clearly on the wedding certificate. This is not paid unless the couple get divorced or the husband dies (it is taken from the estate before distributing it among those who are entitled to inherit from the deceased). This gives the woman some measure of financial security.

The Wedding

Wedding ceremonies differ considerably from one Muslim society to another, and it is not proposed to describe any in detail here. The following information refers to Muslim marriages which are not restricted by non-Muslim laws.

Place: The wedding may take place anywhere, and is often done in the home or the mosque (but not the worship hall).

Officiant: Strictly speaking, the only people necessary are the bride, groom and two adult witnesses. In practice, the local imam is often asked to officiate, and the bride may choose her father to speak for her. Close relatives will also be there, with many other guests from family and friends.

Contract: The essential part of an Islamic wedding is the solemn contract. The bride and groom must agree to this and sign it. It is also signed by the two witnesses. The words will be something like this:

> *The father of the bride:*
>
> *'I marry you my daughter according to Allah's book, the Holy Qur'an and the Sunnah of the Messenger of Allah (P.B.U.H.) with the dowry agreed upon.'*
>
> *The bridegroom replies:*
>
> *'I accept marrying you myself, according to Allah's Book, the Qur'an and the Sunnah of the Messenger of Allah (P.B.U.H.) and with the dowry agreed upon.'*
>
> (ICC leaflet by Dr Sayyed Darsh)

Prayers may be said for Allah's blessing on the marriage, and passages from the Qur'an recited.

Celebrations: These follow, according to custom, with many traditions to wish the couple good luck in their new life together. There will be a marriage feast for all the guests (but without alcohol).

Husband and Wife

The bride will go to live with her husband and his family. It is the husband's responsibility to protect and provide for his wife (since a woman's biological make-up means that any career she has will be restricted by child-bearing). With a man's responsibilities comes also a certain measure of privilege, laid down in the Qur'an:

> *Men are the ones who support women since God has given some persons advantages over others, and because they spend their wealth (on them).*
>
> (Qur'an 4:34)
>
> *Women have the same (rights in relation to their husbands) as are expected in all decency from them; while men stand a step above them.*
>
> (Qur'an 2:228)
>
> (The Qur'an. Basic Teachings, p. 202)

So the husband has the final say in all major decisions, even though the wife will have a lot of influence in the home. Muslims will argue that this is necessary for an orderly existence, but in practice it usually means that the wife has to do a lot of giving, as is shown in the statement from the Islamic Cultural Centre in London, over the page.

Muslim couples are encouraged to have children, as this is natural and is therefore seen to be in accordance with Allah's laws. It is also considered natural for women to bring up the children; and many Muslim women do not work outside the home.

Contraception is not generally encouraged, but most Muslim societies permit its use because Muhammad allowed contraception if there was a good reason for it. The family might not be able to afford any more children or the mother's health might be at risk.

Abortion, on the other hand, is strictly forbidden in Islam, except in rare cases where the mother's life is endangered. Children are considered a blessing from Allah, and to terminate a pregnancy would be regarded as killing a life which Allah has given.

A husband's rights over his wife

1 The wife has to obey the orders of her husband insofar as they are lawful.

2 She has never under any circumstances to betray her integrity both in chastity and in financial affairs.

3 She must refrain from any act which would cause him pain, for example, she should not frown in his presence.

Her outward appearance should be pleasant to him. Such duties of a wife may be construed from a Hadith where it is reported that the Prophet has said: 'The best among wives is the one who appears pleasant to her husband's sight and the one when she is ordered obeys, and the one when he is absent respects his absence in regard to her person and in his money.'

4 Obedience to her husband and acknowledgement of his rights are equal to Jihad in the way of Allah. Disobedience and denial of his rights leads to Hell.

5 A wife must not deny her husband his conjugal rights nor fast superogatorially except with his permission, and cannot give away anything belonging to him except by his permission.

6 She must not leave his house except with his permission and never let any man enter into the house except with his permission.

7 She must take care of the home as Fatimah, daughter of Rasul Allah used to do.

8 The husband's duty towards his wife is to maintain her and procure for her, her needs.

A **fatwa**, i.e. the formal statement of authoritative opinion by a **mufti** (Muslim lawyer). (ICC Newsletter, No. 3)

Polygamy

According to Islamic teaching, men are allowed to marry up to four wives; but women may only have one husband. Muhammad himself is said to have had 12 wives during the last part of his life, although he was married to Khadijah alone for the first 24 years of his married life. In Muhammad's time, polygamy was a good way of providing for the widows, when many young husbands were killed in battle.

Today, polygamy is not very common among Muslims, for a number of reasons. The first wife can write a clause into the marriage contract, insisting that she should remain the only wife. Polygamy is expensive, not only to keep a number of wives, but also to pay their dowries. Also, the Qur'an advises men to have only one wife unless they can be sure to treat all their wives equally (which is virtually impossible):

... then marry such women as may seem good to you, two or three or four (at a time). If you fear that you will not act justly, then (marry) one woman (only) or someone your right hand controls. That is more likely to keep you from committing an injustice.

(Qur'an 4:3)

You will never manage to deal equitably with your wives no matter how eager you may be (to do so) ...

(Qur'an 4:129)

(The Qur'an. Basic Teachings, p. 201)

Divorce

Divorce is disliked, but is permitted, and is relatively easy (at least for men) under Islamic law. Muhammad said that divorce was the most hateful of permitted things and Muslim couples should try to be reconciled before making any final decisions about splitting up. Their families usually do their best to keep the marriage going, since they were the ones who had arranged it in the first place. If the couple cannot work things out, they should get two arbitrators to help, one to represent each party.

If the couple do decide to get a divorce they must wait three months to see whether or not the woman is pregnant, since the husband must provide for the children of the marriage. On divorce, the marriage dowry must be paid up in full, unless it was the woman who wanted the divorce and was at fault. Generally, Muslim women can ask for divorce only if they have had this right written into their marriage contract.

Divorce is regarded as very serious because marriage and the family provide the framework for Islamic life. Islam only allows it because it accepts human nature and recognises that a marriage relationship may not work. It is considered preferable to divorce and remarry than to be forced to continue with an unhappy marriage and perhaps be tempted to commit adultery. Adultery is seen as a far worse threat to society; Saudi Arabia and Iran impose the death penalty for it on married people, in accordance with Shari'ah.

The essential part of the Muslim wedding ceremony is signing the contract.

Muslim Marriage in Britain

Wherever Muslims live, they must obey the laws of that country on marriage and divorce. Many Muslims live in countries where family law is based on the Shari'ah; but others find themselves subject to non-Islamic laws, especially those Muslims living in the West.

In Britain, for example, polygamy is illegal. So, if a Muslim already has a wife, he cannot marry any more wives in Britain. If, however, he has legally married more than one wife abroad, there is nothing to stop him living with all his wives in Britain, but only his first wife will be entitled in any legal benefits.

Divorce is subject to British law, although Muslim immigrants could return to their homeland for a divorce, which would then be recognised in Britain.

The lowest age of sex and marriage in Britain is 16, but it is often lower than this in Muslim countries. Muslims are not allowed to live in Britain with younger brides whom they have married abroad.

Activities

Key Elements

1 Which three of the following are permitted in Islam: contraception, abortion, adultery, divorce, polygamy?
2 What is the essential part of an Islamic wedding?
3 Why are Muslims encouraged to marry young?
4 Why is the dowry important for a Muslim bride?
5 Why do most Muslim men have only one wife?
6 Why is divorce permitted in Islam?

Think About It

7 Give arguments *either* for *or* against arranged marriage, listing your arguments in the order in which you think they are most persuasive.
8 Islam teaches that the right place for sex is within marriage. How do you think Muslim parents would defend this point of view? Present the arguments which they might make *either* to their young teenage daughter, *or* to their young teenage son.
9 What justifications are there for expecting the husband to be the breadwinner and the wife to be the home-maker? Do you think there are any situations where it would be acceptable or preferable for these roles to be shared or reversed?

The Elderly

It is customary for a Muslim wife to live with her husband's family – and for their sons to bring home their wives. In an extended family like this, everyone contributes to family life and everyone is provided for. As people grow old, especially, they need to be cared for; there are many passages in the Qur'an and Hadith encouraging people to look after their parents in their old age.

Nadia (the girl who wrote the book about fasting, which was quoted on p. 49), now 13, is asked: 'Can you think of any aspect of Islam or Muslim family life that you would like others to know about?' This is how she replied:

'*Respect for older people in the family is something that I think is a good idea. I also don't think that by the time you're 16 you're really an adult and able to move away from home. In a Muslim family we keep together and support each other, perhaps much more than some families from other cultures. I don't know what my friends think about older people but certainly in a Muslim family I wouldn't dare to be rude to my parents or grandparents. We talk things over and come to a compromise.*'

(RE Today)

Death Rituals

Dying

When a Muslim is dying, the family gathers round to read the Qur'an and say prayers. The dying person should affirm his or her faith, by saying the familiar words of the Kalimah:

There is no god but Allah,
and Muhammad is the Messenger of Allah.

If the person is unable to say this, it will be recited by someone else there.

Preparing the Corpse

The dead body is washed at least three times. This is done either by the spouse or by someone of the same gender. The first parts of the body to be washed are those which are washed before prayer. The hair (and beard) is perfumed, and also the parts of the body which touch the floor in prostration: the forehead, nose, palms of the hands, knees and feet. The body is wrapped in a shroud: three pieces of white cloth for a man, five for a woman. Alternatively, the ihram may be used if the dead person had completed the Hajj. The face is left uncovered. All this may be done at the mosque if there is a mortuary there.

The funeral prayer (Salah al-Janazah)

The burial takes place as soon as possible after death. This is done out of respect for the dead, particularly in hot countries where the body can quickly decay. It also has the effect of concentrating the grief felt by the bereaved into a relatively short period, rather than upsetting them all over again if the burial is

delayed. Usually only men attend the funeral, as it is thought that women might become too emotional. The body is taken either to the mosque or to the cemetery for the funeral prayer. The men line up behind the imam and pray standing, asking for Allah's forgiveness for the dead person's sins. This is important, if the person is to go to heaven.

Burial

Cremation is forbidden in Islam because Muslims expect Allah to raise up their bodies from the graves on the Last Day. The body is therefore buried. It is laid in the grave with the head turned to the right side, facing Makkah. In hot, dry countries, a coffin is not necessary. Where a coffin is used, the lid is left off if the law permits this. As the grave is filled in with handfuls of earth, passages from

the Qur'an are recited. With the first three handfuls the following verse of the Qur'an is spoken in Arabic:
Most Muslims are allowed only a mound of

Out of the earth We created you,
and We shall restore you into it
and bring you forth from it a second time.

(Arberry) *(Qur'an 20:57)*

earth and a simple headstone to mark the burial place. Shi'is have more elaborate graves.

As the mourners walk from the grave, it is a practice to turn and recite the Kalimah again, to make sure the dead person does not forget his or her religion. It is believed that two angels will come to take charge of the dead person's soul until the Day of Resurrection. They will ask three questions:

'Who is your God?'

'Who is your Prophet?'

'What is your religion?'

Mourning

Muslims should not make too much of their grief, since they should trust in Allah's promises of an after-life and show their acceptance of his will. The period of mourning is no more than three days.

Muslims seek strength from the Qur'an during their bereavement, and pray for the dead person. A common prayer is this:

Peace be upon you; may Allah forgive us all. You went to him before us and we will follow you.

(Milestones, p. 120)

Another common saying, when thinking of the dead, is from the Qur'an:

We belong to Allah, and to him we return.

(Qur'an 2:156)

This shows that Muslims are taught to trust in Allah's goodness, and to accept death as a stage in their life and not the end of it.

Activities

Key Elements

1 Why is the **Khalimah** important to the dying Muslim?
2 What is unusual about the funeral prayer, compared to the performance of salah at other times?

3 How might you recognise a Muslim area in a cemetery in Britain?
4 Why are bereaved Muslims not supposed to grieve too much?

Think About It

5 What would you say is the attitude of your society to the elderly? Give examples.
6 Give arguments to support the view

that the elderly should be cherished and valued.
7 How important do you think it is to grieve the death of a loved one?

Further Information
Major Injunctions in Islam

Say: Come, I will recite what your Lord has forbidden you:

1 *Do not associate anything with Him;*
2 *And (show) kindness towards (your) parents.*
3 *Do not kill your children because of poverty; We shall provide for you as well as for them.*
4 *Do not indulge in shameful acts, be they open or secret.*
5 *Do not kill any person whom God has forbidden, except through [due process of] law.*
   He has instructed you in this so that you may reason.
6 *Do not approach an orphan's wealth before he comes of age, except to improve it.*
7 *Give full measure and weight in all fairness. We do not assign any person more than he can cope with.*

8 *Whenever you speak, be just; even though it concerns a close relative.*
9 *Fulfil God's covenant.*
   Thus has he instructed you so that you may bear it in mind.
10 *This is My Straight Road, so follow it and do not follow (other) paths which will separate you from His Path.*

Thus has He instructed you so that you may do your duty.

(Qur'an 6:151–3)

The Qur'an: Basic Teachings p. 135

The above verses give just one example of the general range of the beautiful teachings, injunctions and recommendations for good conduct and morality contained in the Shari'ah. There are many other examples in the Qur'an and in the teachings of the Prophet Muhammad (blessings of Allah and peace be upon him).

(The Muslim Guide, pp. 30–1)

Further Information
Caring for Parents

Muslims are encouraged to care for their parents, as is shown in this daily reading from the Qur'an and commentary on it.

Your Lord has decreed that you worship none but Him and that you are kind to your parents. Whether one or both of them reaches old age in your life, do not speak a word of contempt, nor reject them, but address them in terms of honour.

And out of kindness, lower to them the wing of humility and say: 'Oh My Lord, bestow on them Your mercy even as they cherished me in childhood.'

(Qur'an 17:23–4)

Human relationships in Islamic society are based on mutual care and benefit, not least

with the family. It is as important a legal duty for children to respect and obey their parents and to care for them when they become old and weak as it was for their parents to care for them when they were young and weak. This respect and honour in no way impedes our total submission to Allah. It is a command from Him and a gesture of submission to Him.

Within the experience of selfless parental love and care is the echo of Divine Love which maintains and cherishes us and which we can never repay, but for which we can only try to show gratitude. It is a Sign to help us understand the relationship we have with our Guardian-Lord. If we cannot manage to show gratitude and honour to those on earth who have given us so much and love us so dearly, we shall surely fail in gratitude to Him whose love and care for us is above all and without limit.

(The Essential Teachings of Islam, pp. 195–6)

Vocabulary

Give the Arabic words for the following:

1. the celebrations held for a baby of seven days old
2. servant
3. obligatory
4. permitted
5. forbidden
6. title of the phrase 'In the name of God, the Merciful, the Compassionate.'
7. Islamic school
8. wedding dowry

Assignments

1 Birth

a) Make a list of at least ten suitable Muslim names (half for girls, and half for boys).

b) Explain why these names are suitable and, where possible, the meaning of each name.

c) Try to imagine how parents feel when, after a long pregnancy and the worries of childbirth, their baby finally arrives. Are any of these emotions expressed through the Muslim birth rituals that are described here? Are any other thoughts or feelings expressed?

2 Education

Try to find some news-cuttings on the debate about Islamic schools in Britain. (Or write, enclosing a s.a.e., to the Muslim Education Co-ordinating Council UK, at the address shown on the letter-heading, p. 96.) Use your information to help with the following questions:

a) Describe the important elements in Islamic education.

b) Explain why many Muslims in the West want special Islamic schools for their children.

c) What arguments can be made against having special Islamic schools in Britain?

3 Dress

Either:

a) Find out what Muslim men and women wear in different countries. Record this in some way.

b) Explain how these costumes comply with Islamic regulations.

c) What is a typical 'Women's Lib.' argument against Muslim women having to be veiled? How far do you agree with this argument?

Or:

a) Draw or cut out from a magazine a picture of a Western teenage girl in clothes which would be perfectly acceptable to Westerners but not to Muslims.

b) Explain why Muslims would object to it.

c) Do you think Western women's dress can sometimes give men the wrong message?

4 Marriage

a) Describe the details of a Muslim wedding ceremony from any one Muslim country.

b) Explain the meaning of each part of the ceremony, and of any symbols used.

c) Which of the ideas expressed about marriage in b) do you think are most important? Say why. Are there any ideas which you disagree with? Give your reasons.

5 Death

a) Write a concise, detailed paragraph describing what is done when a Muslim dies.

b) Explain the reasons for each of the points you have made in your paragraph.

c) How far do you think Islamic teaching about life after death is a comfort to the bereaved? (Look back to Chapter 4 for more information on this.)

6 Muslim Teenagers in Britain

a) You do not need to be told about the difficulties which Muslims face when they live in a non-Muslim society like Britain. If you think carefully, you can work it out for yourself from the information in this chapter. Think particularly about the problems which Muslim *teenagers* might have; express this information in a diagram or table.

b) What are the main reasons for these difficulties? Explain, with examples.

c) What could be done to help Muslim teenagers in Britain?

Appendix of Artefacts

Appendix of artefacts

Islamic artefacts can often be bought at shops at mosques and elsewhere. There are also mail order companies specialising in artefacts for Religious Education, such as Articles of Faith and Religion in Evidence (see Useful Addresses).

The following list shows approximate prices for 1997, showing that it is possible to compile a basic Islamic box for about £30.00.

Prayer mat	£10.00
Compass	£4.00
(Prayer mat with compass attached	£13.50)
Arabic Qur'an	from £6.00
Qur'an stand	£6.00
Prayer cap	£2.00
Prayer beads	£2.50
Arabic postcard	25p
Id card	50p

N.B. Religious artefacts should be treated with respect, since they are the genuine articles used by the faith communities. It would cause particular offence to Muslims if the Arabic Qur'an were treated disrespectfully.

Useful Addresses

Articles of Faith
Bury Business Centre, Kay Street
Bury, Lancashire BL9 6BU

Birmingham Mosque Trust Ltd
180 Belgrave Road, Birmingham 12

Centre for the Study of Islam and
Christian–Muslim Relations
Selly Oak Colleges, Birmingham B29 6LQ

IQRA Trust
24 Culross Street London W1Y 3HE

Islamic Book Centre
120 Drummond Street, London NW1

Islamic Council of Europe
16 Grosvenor Crescent, London SW1 7EP

Islamic Information Service Ltd
Trafalgar House, Waterloo Place, London
SW1

Muslim Aid (charity assisting Muslims in
developing countries)
PO Box 3, London N7 9LR

Minaret House
9 Leslie Park Road, Croydon CR0 6TN

Muslim Education Co-ordinating Council UK
Chairman: Mr Nazar Mustafa
49 Kilmartin Avenue, London SW16, 4RA

Muslim Information Service
233 Seven Sisters Road, London N4 2DA

Religion in Evidence
Monk Road, Alfreton, Derbyshire DE55 7RL

The Islamic Cultural Centre and London
Central Mosque
146 Park Road, London NW8 7RG

The Islamic Foundation
223 London Road, Leicester LE2 1ZE

The Muslim Educational Trust
130 Stroud Green Road, London N4 3RZ

References

The following have been quoted in this book:

A Guide to Hajj, Umrah and Visitat to the Prophet's Mosque (1983) Printed and distributed by Presidency of Islamic Research, Ifta and Propagation, Riyadh Kingdom of Saudi Arabia Trust

Alive to God, Muslim and Christian Prayer Kenneth Cragg

Eid Mubarak (1984) Nadia Bakhsh. Cheetah Books, Essex

First Primer of Islam (1985) Muslim Educational Trust, Surrey

ICC Newsletter No. 36, January 1988 (from p. 4) p. 52 LCM programme for Ramadan 1988

ICC Newsletter No. 40, May 1988 (from p. 55)

ICC Newsletter No. 3, April 1985 (from p. 101)

Islam. Sawm and Hajj (1986) Primary RE Materials. Centre for the Study of Islam and Christian–Muslim Relations, and the Midlands Regional RE Centre

Islamic Cultural Centre (ICC) Newsletter (1988) Sheikh Khalifa, Extracts from 'Friday Khutba', *ICC Newsletter No. 43*, 15 July 1988

Milestones. Rites of Passage in a Multi-Faith Community (1984) C. Collinson and C. Miller. Edward Arnold, London

New Internationalist (1985) Harfiyah Ball, 'The Qur'an', June 1985

Ramadan and Id-ul-fitr (1982) Janis Hannaford. RMEP The Living Festival Series

Religious Studies, A Glossary of Terms, GCSE (1986) Secondary Examinations Council and Religious Education Council of England and Wales

RE Today (1988) Imam Abdul Jalid Sajid interviewed by Michael Hickman in 'Profile', Spring 1988

Daily Readings from the Sacred Texts: Selection from Hadith 3rd Ed (1987) Abdul Hamid Siddique. Islamic Book Publishers, Kuwait

The Art of the Muslim World, Colouring Book 2 Ta-Ha Book Publishers Ltd, London

The Eid ul Fitr Book Multi-Cultural Education Centre, Bristol

The Essential Teachings of Islam (1987) Eds K. Brown and M. Palmer. A Rider Book, Century Hutchinson Ltd, London

The Koran Interpreted (1964) A. J. Arberry. Oxford University Press, Oxford

The Meaning of the Glorious Koran (1976) M. M. Pickthall. Allen & Unwin, London

The Muslim Guide (1986) M. Y. McDermott and M. M. Ahsan. The Islamic Foundation, Leicester

The Prophet Muhammad's Last Sermon Poster. Ta-Ha Publishers Ltd, London

The Qur'an, Basic Teachings (1979) T. B. Irving, K. A. Ahmad and M. M. Ahsan. The Islamic Foundation, Leicester

RE Today, Autumn 1986, (from p. 104)

RE Today, Spring 1988, p. 9 (from p. 6)

Selection from Hadith (1979) Abdul Hamid Siddique. Islamic Book Publishers

The Statesman's Year Book (annually) Macmillan, London

The Times (1987) 'Early rising on the home front', William Greaves in 'Spectrum', 17 August 1987

Third Primer of Islam (1973) Muslim Educational Trust, London

Towards Islam (1977/8) Four essays by Alistair Duncan. The World of Islam Festival Trust

Understanding Islam at GCSE (1989) Jan Thompson. Edward Arnold

Arabic Word List

'Abd lit. 'servant' – often used as the first part of a name, for example, 'Abdullah
adhan first call to prayer
Akhirah life after death
al-Amin 'the Trustworthy' – a name given to Muhammad when he was a young man
al-hamdu-li-Llah 'All praise be to Allah'
Allah 'The God' – the Muslim name for God
Allah Subhana wa Ta'ala 'Allah, Glorified and Exalted'
Allahu Akbar 'Allah is the Greatest' – the devotional phrase most frequently on Muslim lips
Aqiqah birth celebrations
Asr the late afternoon prayer
As-Salamu-Alaykum 'Peace be with you' – a common Muslim greeting
Ayatollah lit. 'Sign of Allah' – title of a leader of the Twelver Shi'is

Bismillah (variant: **Basmalah**) 'In the name of Allah' – the beginning of a phrase which starts all the chapters of the Qur'an except the ninth

caliph 'successor' to Muhammad

Dar-ul-Islam lit. 'House of Islam' – the Muslim empire
Dar-ul-Uloom 'House of Knowledge' – an Islamic college
Dawud David
dhikr 'remembrance' – repetition of the name of Allah

Dhul-Hijjah twelfth month of the Islamic calendar, the pilgrimage month
du'a lit. 'asking' – personal prayer

Fajr the dawn prayer
fard obligatory
Fatihah lit. 'Opening' – title of the first chapter of the Qur'an

Hadith lit. 'statement' – collection of authenticated reports of what Muhammad said, did or approved
hafiz a man who has learnt the whole Qur'an by heart
hafizah a woman who has learnt the whole Qur'an by heart
Hajj lit. 'to set out for a definite purpose' – name of the Greater Pilgrimage to Makkah, the Fifth Pillar of Islam
hajja a woman who has completed Hajj
hajji a man who has completed Hajj
halal permitted
Hanif lit. 'one who is inclined', i.e. to believe in the One God, a monotheist
haram forbidden/sacred
Hijrah 'Emigration' of the Muslims to Yathrib/Madinah and the beginning of the Islamic calendar

Ibrahim Abraham
id festival
idi a festival gift
Id-ul-Adha 'Great Festival', the Festival of Sacrifice
Id-ul-Fitr 'Festival of Fast Breaking' at the end of Ramadan

iftar meal which breaks the fast

ihram lit. 'consecration' – name for the pilgrim's clothes

ijma consensus of Islamic scholars

imam lit. 'in the front' – the prayer leader (who stands in front of the other worshippers)

Imam title for the leader of the Shi'is

Injil Gospel

Insha Allah 'If Allah is willing'

'iqamah second call to prayer, just before prayer begins

'Isa Jesus

Isha the night prayer

Islam the religion of Muslims, meaning 'peace' through 'submission' to Allah

Isra' wal Mi'raj the Night Journey and Ascension of Muhammad into heaven

Jibreel Gabriel

jihad lit. 'striving', i.e. against evil; holy war

jinn a spirit said to live in natural places like springs, trees and caves

Jumu'ah lit. 'assembly' or 'congregation'; the Jumu'ah prayer is the Friday midday prayer

Ka'bah lit. 'cube' – the name of the cube-shaped building in the centre of the Sacred Mosque at Makkah, believed to be the first house of worship of the One God.

Kalimah 'statement' of faith – refers to the First Pillar of Islam

khatib preacher of the Friday sermon

khutbah the Friday sermon

Laylat-ul-Qadr the Night of Power when Muhammad is said to have received his first revelation of the Qur'an

madrasah Islamic school or college

Maghrib the sunset prayer

Mahdi the divinely 'guided' one expected to appear before the Day of Judgement

mahr wedding dowry paid by the bridegroom

Makkah (variant: **Mecca**) the holiest city for Muslims

masjid lit. 'place of prostration', i.e. a mosque

Masjid al Haram the Sacred Mosque in Makkah

Maulid ul Nabi Birthday of the Prophet

mihrab alcove in a wall of a mosque to indicate the direction for prayer

minbar the raised preaching platform in a mosque

minaret tower near or attached to a mosque, from which the call to prayer is sounded

mubarak happy, as in the festival greeting *Eid Mubarak*

muezzin the person who sounds the prayer call

Muharram first month of the Islamic calendar

Musa Moses

Muslim lit. 'one who surrenders' to Allah – a follower of Islam

nabi prophet

niyyah lit. 'intention' – concentrating the mind in preparation for worshipping Allah

qiblah the 'direction' for prayer, facing towards the Ka'bah

qiyam standing (in prayer)

Qur'an lit. 'recitation' – name of the holy book of Islam, believed to have been revealed through Muhammad, who recited it to others

rak'ah a cycle or unit of prayer, both words and actions

Ramadan ninth month of the Islamic calendar, the month of fasting

rasul messenger of Allah, i.e. a prophet who brought a book

ruku bowing (in prayer)

sadaqah voluntary charity

sahih lit. 'sound' – referring to Hadith

Sa'y ritual 'Running' between Mounts As-Safa and Al-Marwa, on pilgrimage

sajdah prostrating (in prayer)

salah ritual prayer to be done five times a day, the Second Pillar of Islam

Salah al-Janazah the funeral prayer

salam 'peace' – final movement in the rak'ah

sawm 'fasting' in the month of Ramadan, the Fourth Pillar of Islam

Shahadah 'declaration' of faith, the First Pillar of Islam

Shari'ah   Islamic law based on the Qur'an and Sunnah

Shi'is   a minority of Muslims, who belong to the 'party' of 'Ali

shirk   sin of idolatry

subhah   prayer-beads

Subhan Allah   'Glory be to Allah'

suf   wool – perhaps where the Sufis got their name

Sunnah   the 'way' or 'custom' of the Prophet, i.e. the example he set for Muslims to follow

Sunni   the majority of Muslims, who claim to follow the right 'path' of Islam

surah   chapter of the Qur'an

tawhid   the oneness of Allah

Tawaf   ritual 'Circling' of the Ka'bah

'ulama   religious lawyers

Ummah   the world-wide Muslim community

'Umrah   the Lesser Pilgrimage to Makkah, which can be done at any time

wudu   ritual washing before prayer

Zabur   the book of Psalms

Zakah   poor-due, the Third Pillar of Islam

Zakat-ul-Fitr   the poor-due at Id-ul-Fitr

Zuhr   the noon prayer

Index